THERAPY WITH
STEPFAMILIES

BRUNNER/MAZEL
BASIC PRINCIPLES INTO PRACTICE SERIES
Series Editor: Natalie H. Gilman

The *Brunner/Mazel Basic Principles Into Practice Series* is designed to present—in a series of concisely written, easily understandable volumes—the basic theory and clinical principles associated with a variety of disciplines and types of therapy. These volumes will serve not only as "refreshers" for practicing therapists, but also as basic texts on the college and graduate level.

BRUNNER/MAZEL
BASIC PRINCIPLES INTO PRACTICE SERIES
VOLUME 6

THERAPY WITH STEPFAMILIES

EMILY B. VISHER, Ph.D.

AND

JOHN S. VISHER, M.D.

BRUNNER/MAZEL, *Publishers* • NEW YORK

Library of Congress Cataloging-in-Publication Data

Visher, Emily B.
    Therapy with stepfamilies / Emily B. Visher and John S. Visher.
        p.   cm.—(Brunner/Mazel basic principles into practice
    series; v. 6)
    Includes bibliographical references and index.
    ISBN 0-87630-799-3 (pbk.)
    1. Family psychotherapy.   2. Stepfamilies—Psychological aspects.
  I. Visher, John S.   II. Title.   III. Series.
  RC488.5.V564   1996
  616.89' 156—dc20   96-1116
                                                                           CIP

Copyright © 1996 by Brunner/Mazel, Inc.

Published by
BRUNNER/MAZEL, INC.
19 Union Square West
New York, New York 10003

Manufactured in the United States of America
10   9   8   7   6   5   4   3   2   1

CONTENTS

PREFACE

When our first book, *Stepfamilies: A Guide to Working with Stepparents and Stepchildren*, was published in 1979, there were few books and scarcely any research studies about remarriage family relationships. Much was being studied and written about the process of divorce, but the next phase in the lives of many widowed and divorced individuals had not yet received attention.

Since that time, however, considerable scholarly and research interest has been focused on this important life-cycle stage, and a large body of clinical experience has accumulated from work with these special families. At first, the research compared stepfamilies to first-marriage families, and stepfamilies were considered to be "an alternative family form" that was deficient and second rate. Then, as stepfamily numbers grew and research studies became more sophisticated, researchers moved away from a "deficit model" comparison with nuclear families toward a more valuable approach for clinicians as well as for the families themselves. The trend now is to seek answers to questions concerned with ways in which to deal effectively with the initial challenges of this more complex family system and move toward successful family integration. The information presented throughout this book comes from these research findings as well as from clinical observation and personal contacts with numerous therapists and stepfamily members from all sections of the country.

Our previous book for therapists, *Old Loyalties, New Ties: Therapeutic Strategies with Stepfamilies,* was based on ten years of giving workshops for therapists in many sections of the United States, plus many contacts with families themselves through the Stepfamily Association of America. This new book incorporates basic ideas from our earlier books, our writing and research published during the last seven years, and our present thinking about stepfamily dynamics and issues concerning clinical work with these families.

Since demographers are predicting that by the year 2010 stepfamilies will be the most prevalent type of family in the United States, it is not surprising that stepfamily members constitute a significant proportion of the clients of therapists, counselors, and social agencies. Because of the therapeutic and dynamic differences between working with stepfamilies and working with other types of families, professionals who work with family problems are seeking more background and expertise in stepfamily therapy, and more and more professional training programs are including stepfamily dynamics as an important part of family therapy courses. We have written *Therapy With Stepfamilies* with this need for basic stepfamily information and guidance in mind. The book is presented in a concise manner, with many case vignettes, plus suggested readings for those wishing additional information in particular areas. Since we consider "family therapy" to refer to a state of mind rather than to the physical presence of all family members in the office, the book can be valuable to professionals with various theoretical backgrounds.

The first two chapters in this book outline helpful ways in which to conceptualize stepfamily dynamics and structure, with examples of the specific tasks that arise for

stepfamilies because of this structure. Chapter 3 empha-
sizes the differences in working therapeutically with remarriage family members compared to those in other types
of families. Chapter 4 focuses on eight major areas of
difficulty for stepfamilies, and Chapter 5 presents helpful
interventions to use when working with families challenged by one or more of these areas of difficulty. Chapter
6 offers therapists many suggestions for helping parents
and stepparents to understand and interact more effectively with their children, and the book ends with a
chapter on successful stepfamilies, including numerous
comments and suggestions from members of those families. A list of resources for stepfamilies and additional
references for therapists are included at the end of the
book.

We have chosen to continue working in the stepfamily
area because of the challenges we experience in becoming
fully aware of subtle nuances in the dynamics of remarriage family systems. In our research we have been most
fortunate to have the encouragement and expertise of
many stepfamilies, colleagues, and friends. We are especially indebted to Anne Bernstein, Lee Combrinck-Graham,
Patricia Papernow, Kay Pasley, Bernard Mazel, and Froma
Walsh, as well as the officers and board members of the
Stepfamily Association of America. We wish to acknowledge their help and also to thank the adults and children
who have shared their difficulties and successes in dealing
with complicated stepfamily issues. Finally, we wish to
express our profound thanks and appreciation to our
children and grandchildren who continue to teach us
many valuable stepfamily lessons and who support us
with their love.

1

INTRODUCTION

Societal changes, new biological knowledge, and a shift in marital expectations have all contributed to producing a wide variety of family forms, among them single-parent families, gay and lesbian families, as well as adoptive and foster families. A rapid increase in the divorce rate in nuclear families has produced a growing number of single-parent households, remarriage families, and stepfamilies. Indeed, demographers are predicting that stepfamilies will soon outnumber first-marriage families in America, since 60% of first marriages end in divorce and approximately 75% of divorced individuals do remarry, typically within three to four years.

It is estimated that of all the children born during the 1980s, 45% will experience the divorce of their parents before they are 18 years old, and 35% will actually *live* with a stepparent during those same years (Glick, 1989). This figure includes only the stepfamily households in which the children are considered to *live*. However, many children live with their mothers in single-parent households and spend time in stepfamily households when they are with their fathers, who have remarried. In addition, children have two stepfamily households when parents have divorced and both have remarried. No wonder there are differing figures for the number of American stepfamilies!

Counting adult stepchildren and stepfamily households with children below age 19, Glick postulates that over half

1

of the American population will experience stepfamily living at some time during their lifetime, either as stepchildren, stepparents, stepgrandparents, or parents who have remarried (Glick, 1991).

Although the changes in families may be more pervasive in the United States, similar changes are occurring throughout the world. This is important to note because this refutes the notion that these changes are the result of the special characteristics of our society. We believe that the important advances in technology and the evolution in our thinking about the dignity and worth of all human beings underlie these changes in the form of families.

The mobility of families, the reach of radio and television, and the impact of the computer age shatter the simplicity and limited vision of the world of a century ago. And with the increase in the life span, concern about the "quantity" of life has been replaced by a concern about life's "quality." Now parents can expect to have many years ahead of them once the children have grown and become independent, while a century ago a majority of children could expect the death of a parent during their growing years, and parents had only a few years together following the raising of their children.

The most profound change, however, has been the growing conviction that all human beings have fundamental rights to "life, liberty, and the pursuit of happiness." With this new understanding, it does not seem surprising that relationships within the family are going through many changes. And with the growing awareness of family violence, it is to be expected that there will be a corresponding increase in the number of separations and divorces. Family change, along with change in general, brings loss and pain as well as hope and promise. However, with new knowledge and new perspectives, it is impossible to return to the past; we cannot shut the door of our minds and forget what we have learned. We must go on to find new and satisfying family relationships.

Before continuing, a few definitions are in order:

1. *A stepfamily is a household in which there is an adult couple, at least one of whom has a child by a previous relationship.* This, of course, includes households in which children are seldom present, as well as those in which the children live most of the time. It also includes households in which the adults have a committed relationship but are not legally married, and it includes same-sex couples who have adopted a child or come together after one or both have had a child.

    These are situations in which a biological or adoptive parent of a child lives with or marries a person who is not the biological parent of the child. Although there are certainly some differences between these family households, the basic emotional dynamics are similar. Because of the similarity of these fundamental dynamic issues, we will be using this broad interpretation throughout the book without calling attention to its inclusiveness. For example, when we use the word "marriage," it will include adults living together in a committed long-term relationship.

2. *A residential parent* (or *household*) is the parent with whom the child lives most of the time. Usually, but not always, this will be the parent who has custody of the child. "Custody" and "visitation" often suggest negative legal images; because of this we prefer, whenever possible, to use the terms *residential* and *access* when referring to these concepts in stepfamilies.

3. *A nonresidential parent* is the parent with whom the child lives less than the majority of the time.

4. *A remarried parent* is a person with a biological or adoptive child who marries someone other than the child's biological or adoptive parent.

5. *A stepparent* is the new partner of the child's parent. This adult is not biologically related to the child.

Modern dictionaries continue to include negative definitions of "stepchild" and "stepparent," and the "step" prefix continues to carry a negative connotation. In fact, it is so negative for many people that heated arguments arise when someone uses this nomenclature. As a result of attempts to find a more positive term for families of this type many different words have made their appearance. These include: Combined, binuclear, complicated, reconstituted, remarriage or REM families, and blended families. "Reconstituted" reminds individuals of ersatz orange juice, and "blended families" suggests homogenization rather than the integration that allows for the continuation of varied family backgrounds. As Papernow (1991) puts it, "If it is a blended family, someone is getting creamed." Indeed, many people speak of "blended families" and "stepfamilies" in the same sentence. This occurs because they consider blended families to be families in which both adults bring children from previous relationships, and stepfamilies to be households in which only one of the adults brings children from an earlier marriage.

None of these synonyms negate the need to refer to "stepparents" and "stepchildren" for clarity and accuracy. Because of this we continue to use the term "stepfamily," a term that includes all members, even a remarried parent who marries a person with no children and therefore does not become a stepparent. The inclusiveness of "stepfamily" is appreciated by many stepparents whose partners are not also stepparents. For all these reasons we have chosen to use the original prefix "step" (which comes from the old English "steop" meaning orphaned or bereaved) and to try through education to effect at least a neutral emotional acceptance of this term.

Unfortunately, society tends to negatively stigmatize stepfamily households and react to them as inferior and inadequate families (Coleman & Ganong, 1987). The term "stepchild" is used pejoratively as in "the marketing department is seen as the stepchild of the company," while "Bad News About Stepparents" is the title of a section of an article about single parent and stepfamily households (Whitehead, 1993).

A media furor in England portrayed a similar ambience surrounding stepfamilies in that country, a stigma that is even greater in Eastern Europe and still more so in dissimilar cultures. In Great Britain, a mail order company sought to find "the model family for 1994" to pose for illustrations in their catalog, with TV viewers voting for the winner from among the finalists. To quote the *London Daily Mirror's* sensitive account, "Gavin and Michelle look so good together that they were chosen from 100,000 contestants to model clothes for Kay's catalogs.... That would have been the end of their story but for the fact that Michelle had been married before and has a five-year-old daughter (Mia) by her ex-husband.... In a flash their loving relationship was transformed into something perverse and sordid." Michelle said, "We are so ordinary, but suddenly we were held up there to represent the modern British family. We only entered the competition to model clothes, not to say we were anything special."

The *London Sunday Times* carried a very large headline: "Decline and Fall of the Nuclear Family," and many other newspapers also carried extraordinarily negative articles. It is as though the existence of stepfamilies threatens first-marriage families, as though there has to be only one type of family, not a healthy diversity. In view of this, it is not surprising that adults often attempt to hide their stepfamily status and that they react negatively to therapy when they believe their therapist also holds a negative view of remarriage families and is reacting to their family as an inferior and inadequate family.

It is difficult for anyone to flourish in an atmosphere of negativity, and the needs of stepfamilies, despite their prominence in the fabric of American life, have been neglected by society. A harsh environment can retard stepfamily growth and development, and counteracting this unfortunate perception of remarriage families often becomes a primary task of therapy. To be successful, therapy needs to take a view of viable and productive families that goes beyond the model of Mom, Dad, and two children encircled by a white picket fence. Stepfamilies are different from original first-marriage families, not better, not worse, simply different. Instead of being compared negatively with nuclear families, they need understanding and acceptance, with assessment that uses their own norms.

Hopefully, the information throughout this book will provide a framework for working with stepfamilies in a mutually rewarding way.

EFFECTIVE STEPFAMILY THERAPY

A recent large study of stepfamily therapy (Pasley, Rhoden, Visher, & Visher, 1996) gives valuable insights into what the respondents found to be the most helpful interventions in their therapy. Two hundred sixty-seven questionnaires were returned from stepfamily couples reporting on their experience in stepfamily therapy. Although this sample represents a middle and upper middle class group, predominantly Caucasian, we have found that their responses appear to have validity for more dissimilar groups as well. Families with multiple problems will, however, require more varied and longer-term interventions.

The information that follows comes from clients' answers to these questions:

- What three things during therapy stand out as the most helpful to your therapy experience?
- What was the single most important factor, whether or not related to therapy, that brought stability to your family?
- Was there something about the therapy experience that you found not helpful to you? If yes, please tell us what was not helpful.
- Why do you believe this was not helpful?

Eighty-three percent of respondents reported positive therapeutic experiences, and 51% reported negative aspects of their therapy. In a number of cases, families had seen several therapists before finding one who was helpful to them. In addition to responses commenting on the importance of a therapist possessing good basic skills, stepfamily adults reported four types of specific interventions as being especially useful:

1. Validating and normalizing stepfamily dynamics
2. Supplying important psychoeducation
3. Reducing helplessness
4. Building the couple relationship

Even in multiple-problem stepfamilies, dealing with the stepfamily issues in these ways enhances the member's ability to deal with the other difficulties. A few typical comments illustrate the importance of each of these significant areas. Further discussion and therapeutic examples are given in Chapter 5, in which these and 12 other specific interventions are presented in some detail.

Validating and Normalizing Stepfamily Dynamics

This research indicates that validating and normalizing family dynamics is extremely important. Positive interactions help validate the worth of the family, and viewing stepfamily integration as possible and worthwhile can motivate adults to continue working on this usually lengthy process.

When therapists understand, accept, and let their clients know how normal it is to have initial difficulties, their relief can be profound. With reduction in anxiety and increase in self-esteem, stepfamily members are then better able to handle their situation more effectively. Their strong negative emotional reactions may also diminish because they are anticipated and, therefore, are less of a threat.

The adults in one stepfamily commented, "The therapists' attitude toward stepfamilies, their warmth and their
genuine caring is what counts the most." Another said, "It
alleviated the stepmom's guilt. The therapist made it clear
it was not all her fault." And a third wrote, "The therapist
acknowledged that my feelings were legitimate and that I
was not a terrible person for having the feelings that I had."

Supplying Important Psychoeducation

Stepfamily couples typically are bombarded initially by
situations and emotions they have not anticipated. Having
a knowledgeable therapist define their stresses and put
them into a stepfamily perspective often results in imme-
diate improvement, and stepparents and remarried parents say, "What a relief to know we're not alone, and that
the difficulties and what we're feeling is normal. We're not
crazy after all!" Normalizing their situations and validating their emotional reactions is a powerful therapeutic
tool.

Even though numerous books exist now to help stepfamilies, many adults come into therapy having little
knowledge of stepfamily norms. Having a stepfamily road
map can be crucial for successful progress towards integration. Knowing where the trouble spots are and receiving
reliable information to assist in dealing with them are
important elements in stepfamily therapy during the lengthy
integration process. As one respondent wrote, "The three
most important aspects of our therapy were education,
education, and education!"

To be effective in this respect therapists need to be
initially more active and participatory than with first-
marriage families, and they need to be knowledgeable
about stepfamily issues and dynamics. A table listing
stepfamily tasks and suggestions for accomplishing these
tasks is included in Chapter 2.

Many of the therapy questionnaires were returned with
comments pertaining indirectly to psychoeducation as

well as to specific information their therapists had mentioned. For example:

> "We were given realistic expectations."
>
> "It was a safe place to communicate and we learned to be empathetic with each other's position."
>
> "Therapy made my husband realize that a new wife can't automatically love her husband's children as her own."
>
> "The therapist helped the stepparent back off and the husband take charge of his children. Discipline in stepfamilies is different."

Research is indicating that it is the relationships within the household and not the form of the family that leads to satisfactory or unsatisfactory outcomes for adults and children (Pasley, 1987). Identifying the stressful stepfamily situations and offering information about ways to move toward effective solutions can reduce chaos in the family and help the household to settle down.

Reducing Helplessness and Increasing Autonomy

Both the adults and the children in stepfamilies tend to feel overwhelmed and helpless. Children have experienced major wrenching changes in their lives that they have not been able to control, and adults routinely feel pressure from having an ex-spouse and parent of the children in another household with considerable influence on their own household. Not surprisingly, the adults in one household often believe that the solution to their dilemmas lies in making the other household change in some way. If this does not occur or they are not able to control the children's other household, the adults' anger tends to increase their feelings of helplessness and diminish their ability to see positive changes that they can make.

Frequently, new couples are tripping over unrealistic expectations and their sense of helplessness can dissipate with psychoeducation and specific suggestions that help them to understand which areas can be changed and how to proceed. Another important intervention is helping the adults let go of situations they cannot control (e.g, the children's other household) and become active within their own sphere of influence. This clarifies responsibilities and brings more predictability and order into the family.

Assisting adults in allowing their children control over their lives, which is appropriate for their ages and emotional maturity, can reduce the children's need to attempt to gain autonomy in unproductive ways, such as by dawdling, by not accepting household responsibilities given to them, or by not doing their homework. Having a sense of mastery over their day-to-day life is very important to children, and there are usually many opportunities for parents and stepparents to foster this autonomy. In one family, each child could choose the dinner menu one night every week. In another, the stepfather taught his adolescent stepson to drive his car and let the teenager use it when appropriate. When asked what made a positive difference for them during their early years in a stepfamily, young adults often talk about the times they were trusted. Being trusted usually is related to a degree of autonomy for individuals of any age. No wonder the couples mentioned such things as being helpful:

> "We learned that we could control our own household."
>
> "I didn't need to take my stepdaughter's comments personally."
>
> "We learned to get out of the middle and let our children work out their complaints about their mother with her in her household."

Building the Couple Relationship

When they were asked what was the single most important factor in bringing stability to the family, adult stepfamily respondents to the therapy research study overwhelmingly responded that it was the improved bonding between the couple: "We can work as a team now"; "Balancing family time with couple time"; "Husband and wife relationship comes first so we can work as a team"; "My husband made a commitment to me by letting the family know that my leaving was not one of the options."

Remarried parents and their children bring to their new stepfamilies a parent/child alliance that has existed since the birth of the child. This is a powerful and important alliance that needs to be preserved. However, there is now a couple that has been together for a much shorter time and the adults need to strengthen their commitment to one another as they work out ways in which to strengthen the family unit.

As in any type of family, it is the adult or adults in the household who are in charge of the family. If they are not able to work together, smooth functioning of the family is in jeopardy. Many adults in their therapy survey responses said that understanding one another in therapy and having the support and encouragement of the therapist to strengthen their commitment to one another resulted in improved functioning of the entire household.

INEFFECTIVE STEPFAMILY THERAPY

As noted earlier in this chapter, slightly more than half of the research respondents said that aspects of their therapy experience were not helpful and a number spoke of seeing several therapists before finding one who was helpful to them. A few considered that the total experience was negative. For some clients, the difficulty arose because the therapist did not seem warm or skilled as a counselor. For others, the problem occurred because the partner (usually the husband) would not take part in the therapy. However, nearly half of the responses were specific to therapy with remarriage families: The therapist was not knowledgeable about stepfamily issues and dynamics. These responses were clear and direct, and the following illustrate some of the types of nonhelpful interactions mentioned:

"The therapist expected us to feel and act like a nuclear family, and that's a lie."

"She treated us like we were a regular family with children and she had no concept of the bonding problems, the alienation that is felt, or the loyalty problems."

"The therapist talked about bio family discipline styles and they don't work."

"The therapist believed I loved my stepchild when I said I didn't—he couldn't quite get it."

In writing about seeing several therapists, other families made similar comments to this one: "We saw three therapists in five years before we got to one who knew anything *at all* about stepfamilies. Our situation had continued to deteriorate and we couldn't understand what was wrong and why we couldn't be helped."

These comments are to be expected since validation, normalization, and psychoeducation are so important in stepfamily therapy, and as yet few therapy training programs include information on this type of family. Fortunately, this lack is beginning to receive the attention that it deserves. Without stepfamily knowledge, therapists can be ineffective in helping family members build a successful new stepfamily.

In the following chapters, we will clarify the differences between remarriage families and original families, outline what we know about normal reactions, provide important basic stepfamily information, and offer therapeutic suggestions and strategies. References for further reading that will provide a more complete exploration of these topics will be suggested throughout the book and in the Resources section.

2

STEPFAMILY INTEGRATION

We are often asked what we believe to be the greatest problem for adults entering into a remarriage in which children are involved. Our answer is that it is the adults' unrealistic expectation that the household will integrate and settle down relatively quickly. Children appear to be more realistic about this than are adults. One 16-year-old put it very clearly, "It takes me a long time even to make a good friend at school."

Relationships are not developed overnight, and integrating the different expectations and ways of doing things often takes considerable time. What family members bring to the process will, of course, influence the specifics of the process for each individual stepfamily: Younger children are more dependent on the adults and have fewer preconceived ideas of how families "ought" to work than do teenagers; the self-esteem of the parents and their sense of security regarding their relationship with their children affects their ability to deal with their children's other household; former family experiences exert considerable influence, enhancing or retarding the successful integration of the family.

Regardless of these personal characteristics, however, the integration process of stepfamilies in the United States and in similar cultures around the world occurs within families that have important structural characteristics, different from those of first-marriage families. The special tasks that need to be accomplished arise because of these structural characteristics and involve intense and complex emotional issues. These elements can make for initial difficulties and they explain the reasons why stepfamily integration is ordinarily a lengthy and stressful process.

BASIC DIFFERENCES IN STEPFAMILY STRUCTURE

We see seven basic differences between the structural characteristics of remarriage families and first-marriage families in the United States. The first five apply both to stepfamilies in the United States and to other countries as well, while the last two are dependent on the laws and social customs of the specific country (Visher & Visher, 1979). Conscious recognition of these characteristics helps therapists and family members understand the emotions and situations that may arise in the family. Often therapists need to bring these differences to the attention of the family. One father/stepfather said after this was done: "I always knew that, but I didn't *really* know it until you spoke about it."

1. The Family Begins After Many Losses and Changes.

Any marriage involves changes and loss of a familiar pattern of life. With a divorce as well as with a remarriage, losses and changes are magnified: Children are no longer living full time with both of their parents; children as well as adults may have a new residence, school, and neighborhood, as well as unfamiliar foods, rules, and ways of doing things that have replaced familiar patterns for everyone in the family. With a remarriage, the changes become even greater. This can feel to children as though they have lost their family, not simply full-time contact with one or both of their parents.

Another very important loss for children is the loss of attention given to them by their parent who has remarried.

One such parent, when listening to a discussion of the losses for children, responded by saying with sudden awareness, "I lived for three years in a single-parent household with my daughter. When I came home from work each day, I wanted someone to talk to, and I talked to my daughter. I'm remarried now and when I come home at night I talk with my husband." With this recognition, this remarried mother planned to include a conversation with her daughter in her routine when she came home after work.

Parents tend to be more aware of the gains for their children following their remarriage than of the children's losses. It is important to help the adults understand such losses as the need to share their room with stepsiblings or the loss of their place as the oldest child in the family and perhaps as their parent's helper during the single-parent household phase. When the adults understand, they are more able to empathize and communicate with their children. Both adults and children need to acknowledge their losses and let go of the past before they can fully accept and enjoy the gains in their present family.

2. Both Adults and Children Come Together with Incongruent Individual, Marital, and Family Life Cycles.

In an original marriage, two adults become a couple at the same time and become parents at the same time. This does not happen in a stepfamily, where adults and children come together from often markedly dissimilar marital and family experiences.

A man who is the parent of three children may marry a woman who has never had children. He may have no desire to return to a life-cycle stage that includes changing diapers or going to PTA meetings. Yet, at the same time, she begins to long to have a child. Another common scenario is when an older man marries a young woman and they encounter difficulties later on when he retires from

working while she is beginning to enjoy her career and
wishes to continue working. These dilemmas often require considerable therapeutic attention.

3. Children and Adults All Have Expectations from Previous Families.

In a first marriage, two adults each have learned behavior
patterns and values from their families of origin. Children
are born into a family and grow up unconsciously absorb-
ing the values and patterns of the family. In a stepfamily,
the children as well as the adults bring with them values
and ways of doing things from their families of origin, from
previous marriages, and from single-parent households.
Many of the changes in the new household will need to be
discussed and negotiated by family members in order to
try to reach a consensus.

Unfortunately, different ways of doing things often feel
"wrong" and arguments arise. The need is to help the
individuals understand that differences can provide rich-
ness and choice and are not "right" or "wrong." This
allows them to communicate productively about their
differences and make the necessary choices for their family. One family, for example, solved a major disagreement
during their first Christmas together by purchasing one
tree with the understanding that the husband and his
children would decorate one side of the tree in their
accustomed manner with white flocking, small twinkling
lights, and colored ornaments; the wife and her children
would decorate the other half of the tree in their usual way,
green with large colored lights and handmade popcorn
strings and ornaments the children had created over the
years.

At times, former traditions are combined, or one way
may be selected as most desired by all; at other times, new
traditions and ways of doing things become the pattern for
the new household. As in all families, there has to be a

flexibility to accommodate different interests and needs as the children grow and the family evolves.

4. Parent–Child Relationships Predate the New Couple Relationship.

This is the reverse of what transpires in an original marriage where the couple has formed a bond and has an alliance before children are born. In stepfamilies, remarried parents come into the family with preexisting bonds, experiences, and alliances with their children; virtual strangers may suddenly be living together under the same roof.

Remarriages are usually more complex than first marriages because of the need to deal with prior legal and emotional relationships. When the adults have children from a prior relationship, many complexities arise. Considering just the stepfamily household, remarried parents often experience many loyalty conflicts as they attempt to meet the wishes of their children and also of their new partner. This is a difficult task and all too often the importance of the remarried parent role in the family is overlooked as the stepparent is considered to be the cause of the tension in the household and is scrutinized in detail.

We believe that it is essential to view stepfamily dynamics through a systemic lens. Too often, stepparents are seen as playing the pivotal role in whether or not a stepfamily becomes successful. In other types of families, a disturbed and upset member can have a deleterious influence on the functioning of the family; stepfamilies are no different in this respect. However, in remarriage families it is usually the interpersonal, interactional relationships of the adults and the eventual willingness of the children to accept the family changes that are the most significant factors in the functioning of the family.

There are examples of parent and stepparent roles that enhance stepfamily functioning in several sections of the following chapters.

5. There Is a Biological Parent in Another Household or in Memory.

Children usually have strong emotional ties to each of their biological parents, even if one of them has died. Adults both in and outside the family often have difficulty accepting more than two parenting figures in a child's life, and children are often expected to choose among three or four adults. This is an unfortunate situation since research and clinical observation indicate that this is a major cause of continuing adjustment difficulties for children after divorce and remarriage. On the other hand, being permitted and encouraged to form good relationships with all the parenting adults in their lives can magically reduce children's loyalty conflicts and give them more exposure to important adult relationships.

Unfortunately, society is slow to accept the concept of nonantagonistic divorces (Aydintug, 1995). Society has difficulty accepting more than two parenting figures in a child's life, and parents' insecurity and fear of loss of their children's affection is an important factor in sustaining the anger between ex-spouses. Even so, many former spouses are beginning to cooperate rather than compete in raising their children. Therapists can help parents to understand how important they are to their children, and how destructive the continuing competition and anger can be for everyone concerned. As one 10-year-old said to her therapist, "I don't want my stepmother to be a good mother. I want my real mother to be a good mother." This may not always be possible, but the child's words illustrate the importance of parents to their children.

Many children spend time in both their mother's and their father's households. While each household needs to have a boundary of privacy around it, these households are connected through the children. As Weston (1993) puts it, "There needs to be gates in the fences around each house for the children to pass through." In this way, children can maintain contact with both parents. They are not asked to give up a parent because they have acquired a stepparent.

With no access to their other parent, children tend to build unrealistically positive fantasies about that parent, fantasies that cannot be equaled by any stepparent.

Many remarried parents need information and education in this area. They may also need therapeutic help in maintaining appropriate boundaries if the remarried parent's connection with the former spouse is related to the wish to continue an inappropriate relationship rather than to maintaining a connection in the interest of raising their children. In fact, if there is not a sufficient psychological boundary between the children's two households, a pervasive fantasy can be fueled on the part of the children who dream that their two biological parents will get together again.

We believe that additional parenting figures can bring added emotional support for children. Over time, developing a "parenting coalition" of parents and stepparents in the children's two households is often beneficial for the adults as well as for the children. This will be discussed further in Chapters 3 and 4.

6. Children Are Often Members of Two Households.

There is a growing body of research that indicates that after a divorce and a remarriage, children's adjustment and future well-being tend to be more positive if they have regular contact with both of their parents (Hetherington, Stanley-Hagan, & Anderson, 1989). These contacts increase rather than decrease the likelihood that positive stepchild/stepparent relationships will eventually develop. The Resource List at the back of this book contains suggestions for excellent reference books to help parents and stepparents deal with this aspect of stepfamily life.

7. There Is Little or No Legal Relationship Between Stepparents and Stepchildren.

Family law has been unable to keep pace with the rapid changes in family life. Even in the few states that are beginning to recognize the importance of legal support for good stepparent/stepchild relationships, stepparents have only minimal rights (Fine, 1992a). Unfortunately, social and cultural nonacceptance exerts a profoundly negative impact on the lives of many members of remarriage families, often by subjecting children to unnecessary relationship losses following the divorce or death of the children's biological parent. One hopeful sign for stepparents and stepfamilies in the future is that there is a growing interest and concern by family lawyers in studying and responding to the needs of other than first-marriage families.

Sometimes remarried parents and stepparents consider a legal adoption of the children by the stepparent. There are certain families in which this alternative works well, but the decision needs to be given careful attention because it amounts to an important cutoff for children. The adoption may sever the relationship with the parent of the same sex as that of the adopting stepparent, and this can be a serious loss for a child.

The complexity of the issue is illustrated by the following example:

> Kevin's mother and father divorced when he was seven years old. His father remarried a year and a half later, and his mother remarried six months after that. Kevin lived most of the time with his mother and stepfather, but was permitted to see his father and stepmother four to five days each month.
>
> Kevin's mother wished to have him adopted by her husband and a court date was set for the hearing. Both the couples appeared in court with Kevin, who was now 10 years old. The judge asked Kevin if he wanted to be adopted, and he said "Yes." The father gave his consent and the adoption was granted.
>
> Twenty-four years later, Kevin and his second wife sought therapy because of difficulties integrating their stepfamily. When the family chaos had subsided, and when intimacy issues between the couple had been resolved, Kevin chose to remain for several months of

individual therapy. During these months the most important and the most poignant sessions were concerned with his adoption.

After the adoption Kevin had lost touch with his father and he buried his subsequent feelings. He often found that he was depressed. In therapy, Kevin began to remember and talk about that day in court when he was 10. He spoke of not being sure his father and stepmother wanted him to be with them and of being afraid that if he angered his mother by saying "No" to the judge she and her new husband would not want him either. So Kevin had told the judge, "Yes, I want to be adopted by my stepfather."

As Kevin began to cry, the therapist asked, "What were you hoping your father would do?" Through his tears Kevin replied, "I wanted him to say 'No.'" After a period of mourning, Kevin made a decision to try to find his father and to reconnect with him.

Often, the motivation for a stepparent adoption is the adults' attempt to create a "nuclear family." Attempting to create a nuclear family negates the children's original family and robs them of their tie to the past. In other instances, the motivation is to give a child the same surname as the rest of the family. However, this latter goal can be accomplished informally without an adoption, though at times this can be the cause for serious disputes between the child's two biological parents. Clearly, adoption is an important issue that requires very careful attention.

INTEGRATION TASKS RESULTING FROM STEPFAMILY STRUCTURE

All families have the task of providing an environment in which the adults can find satisfaction and in which children can grow and develop into happy and productive adults. Because of the structural characteristics of stepfamilies just discussed, there are a number of specific tasks that need to be accomplished for satisfactory family integration to take place. These tasks, tied to the remarriage structure, are:

1. Dealing with losses and changes
2. Negotiation of different developmental needs
3. Establishing new traditions
4. Developing a solid couple bond
5. Forming new relationships
6. Creating a parenting coalition
7. Accepting continual shifts in household composition
8. Risking involvement despite little support from society

Clinical observation, recent empirical research, and the experience of stepfamilies themselves provide many guidelines for accomplishing these tasks. Exhibit 2.1 (pp. 23–27) delineates the tasks and gives strategies for accomplishing them. This is useful for stepfamily adults and also for therapists in understanding the challenges and learning ways that have been found to be important in working towards these goals. As was mentioned in Chapter 1, clients need to have specific information on how to deal with challenges in the family. Sharing this outline with clients and discussing with them many of the specific steps mentioned in the outline have proven to be very effective. For family members who wish it, this outline appears in the publication *Stepfamilies Stepping Ahead,* which is listed in the Resources section.

Successful stepfamilies have usually made satisfactory progress in achieving these special stepfamily goals (Visher & Visher, 1990; Kelley, 1995). While many of the suggestions need little discussion, others are referred to throughout this book, and still others involving such things as discipline issues, roles for stepparents, and developing a parenting coalition are discussed at some length in the following chapters. Additional information

Exhibit 2.1

GUIDELINES FOR ACCOMPLISHING
STEPFAMILY TASKS

The "bottom line" for stepfamilies is to establish a new family identity. There are a number of tasks (based on the differences between first-marriage families and stepfamilies) that need to be accomplished in order to do this. Some strategies for helping to accomplish each task are suggested. Some tasks are more difficult and it may not be possible to accomplish them all right away.

1. TASK: DEALING WITH LOSSES AND CHANGES

It helps to remember that each person in the family experiences loss, since all change involves letting go of former situations and relationships. Children usually would prefer to remain in their previous family pattern and often get angry and act in annoying ways, rather than crying and feeling sad. Reading books, introducing changes slowly, and helping them to talk about their sadness can make it possible for adults and children to say goodbye to the past and begin to appreciate the gains of the new family unit.

STRATEGIES:
- Identify/recognize losses for all individuals.
- Support expressions of sadness.
- Help children talk about feelings, instead of acting them out.
- Read stepfamily books.
- Make changes gradually.
- See that everyone gets a turn.
- Inform children of plans involving them.
- Accept the insecurity of change.

2. TASK: NEGOTIATE DIFFERENT DEVELOPMENTAL NEEDS

In a remarriage, adults and children are at different places in their lives. One partner may have been married before and the other may have been unmarried; one may have been a parent and the other not yet had children; both may have children but be unfamiliar with or have forgotten what children of certain ages are like; children may be adolescents who have reached an age where they would rather be with their friends than become involved in forming a new family unit. These differences usually mean that some of the needs of the individuals will not fit together easily. As a result, it may take a lot of flexibility and tolerance and talking about these differences to find the best ways of satisfying as many of these needs as possible.

(Continued)

STRATEGIES:

- Take a child development and/or parenting class.
- Accept validity of different life-cycle phases for adults and children.
- Communicate individual needs clearly.
- Negotiate incompatible needs.
- Develop tolerance and flexibility.

3. TASK: ESTABLISHING NEW TRADITIONS

Children and adults have been used to eating certain foods, following certain patterns of activity, and doing a million things in a different way. It's hard not to feel that your way is RIGHT and that the other way is WRONG! Instead, compare notes about the ways that all household members have celebrated holidays and birthdays, what kinds of foods they like, and how everyday events have been handled.

How does everyone want things to go in your present household? Try combining former ways of doing some things perhaps (turkey *and* ham for Thanksgiving), taking turns with others (taking a family drive one Sunday, playing Monopoly the next), and starting new traditions that will become special for your new family.

The couple (and whenever possible, the children, too) need to decide together on the house rules, but stepparents need to form a friendly relationship with their stepchildren before attempting to see that the house rules are followed. The parent of the children needs to set the limits at the beginning.

STRATEGIES:

- Recognize ways are different, not right or wrong.
- Concentrate on important situations only.
- Stepparents take on discipline enforcement slowly.
- Use "family meetings" for problem solving and giving appreciation.
- Shift "givens" slowly whenever possible.
- Retain/combine appropriate rituals.
- Enrich with new creative traditions.

4. TASK: DEVELOPING A SOLID COUPLE BOND

It is easy for adults to spend so much time and energy doing their best to make the household run smoothly that they forget to take care of their own needs for fun and relaxation as a couple. It usually takes active planning ahead for the adults to make time for themselves. Developing and enjoying themselves as a couple is important not only for the couple, but also for the children (although the children may

(Continued)

resent it at first). Children need to have a strong guidance to give them family stability and to teach them how to work together so that when they mature and leave home they will have the skills to form their own successful couple relationships.

STRATEGIES:

- Accept couple as primary long-term relationship.
- Nourish couple relationship.
- Plan for couple "alone time."
- Decide general household rules as a couple.
- Support one another with children.
- Expect and accept different parent/stepparent–child feelings.
- Work out money matters together.

5. TASK: FORMING NEW RELATIONSHIPS

Creating bonds between individuals generally takes considerable time because good relationships are the result of sharing many happy and satisfying times together. Learning about one another and doing things in pairs can help this process. It may be hard for a parent to step back a little so that the stepparent and stepchildren have a chance to be together, but this is one of the best ways to work toward building new relationships. This helps the people in the household to begin to feel like a family group. At times, particularly with older children, strong bonds of caring may not develop. However, a stepparent can be "fair" to stepchildren even when they have not developed a warm relationship.

STRATEGIES:

- Fill in past histories.
- Make stepparent–stepchild one-on-one time.
- Make parent–child one-on-one time.
- Parent make space for stepparent–stepchild relationship.
- Do not expect "instant love" and adjustment.
- Be fair to stepchildren even when caring has not developed.
- Follow children's lead in what to call stepparent.
- Do fun things together.

6. TASK: CREATING A "PARENT COALITION"

Developing a civil relationship between the adults who are involved in raising the children benefits everyone even though there may be very little contact between the adults. Having a neutral business-like relationship can reduce the adults' fears of the children's

(Continued)

acceptance of both parents and stepparents. Even though former marriage relationships may have ended, parent–child relationships continue. Even if contact between divorced parents does not occur very often, effective communication helps the children to feel more loved and increases their self-esteem.

STRATEGIES:

- Deal directly with parenting adults in other households.
- Parents keep children out of the middle.
- Do not talk negatively about parent in other household.
- Control what you can and accept limitations.
- Avoid power struggles between households.
- Respect parenting skills of former spouse.
- Contribute own "specialness" to children.
- Communicate between households in most effective manner.

7. TASK: ACCEPTING CONTINUAL SHIFTS IN HOUSEHOLD COMPOSITION

Getting used to the comings and goings of children can take some time. After awhile, such changes can feel "normal." Do not save all special events for times when nonresident children are present. If you do, the "resident" children may feel that the "nonresident" children are more loved and special. While these changes can upset the routine of the household, they also mean that the adults have a rest from their parenting responsibilities.

STRATEGIES:

- Allow children to enjoy their household.
- Give children time to adjust to household switches.
- Avoid asking children to be "messengers" or "spies."
- Consider a teenager's serious desire to change residence.
- Respect privacy (boundaries) of all households.
- Set consequences that affect only your own household.
- Provide a personal place for nonresident children.
- Plan special times for various household constellations.

8. TASK: RISKING INVOLVEMENT DESPITE LITTLE SUPPORT FROM SOCIETY

Even though they may not have a legal status, stepparent–stepchild relationships can be very rewarding. Children gain by having more adults to care about them, and stepparents gain from the satisfaction of contributing to the children's lives. Even when a stepfamily is disrupted by divorce or the death of a parent, it can be important for stepparents to be active in maintaining these relationships.

(Continued)

STRATEGIES:

- Include stepparents in school, religious, sport, and other activities.
- Give legal permission for stepparent to act when necessary.
- Continue stepparent–stepchild relationships, after death or divorce, when bonds have developed.
- Stepparent include him- or herself in stepchild's activities.
- Find groups supportive of stepfamilies.
- Remember that all relationships involve risk.

---

for therapists is also contained in the book *Old Loyalties, New Ties: Therapeutic Strategies with Stepfamilies* (Visher & Visher, 1988).

Impact of Stepfamily Structure on Basic Emotional Needs

As a rule, in newly formed stepfamilies children and adults experience strong, sometimes even painful, emotions.

One way of understanding the amount of emotional pain and stress is to consider three very important, basic, and universal human needs and the initial deprivation of these needs brought about by the structural characteristics of remarriage families. These needs are the following:

1. The need to belong to a group
2. The need to be cared about and appreciated and to be loved by and have secure attachments to a few special individuals
3. The need for personal control and autonomy in one's life

These are needs shared by individuals of all ages from all cultures (Bohannan, 1993), though individuals in different cultures may satisfy such needs in different ways. In the United States there are many examples of the importance of love and caring, belonging, and autonomy or personal power: groups and cults and the ways in which they satisfy people's hunger to belong; love and caring, the theme of an infinite number of books; numerous psychologically based writings dealing with ways in which it is possible to empower others and also ways in which to gain control over one's own life. These needs are powerful indeed, and their opposites—alienation, helplessness, rejection, and loss of love—cause deep pain and suffering.

Unfortunately, the structure of remarriage families initially makes the satisfaction of these basic needs virtually impossible. Stepfamily members experience many losses and changes, and in various degrees also have feelings of strangeness and lack of control that arise from living with unfamiliar people in strange surroundings. In new stepfamilies, strangers may come together under one roof and try to live together. Even when the individuals have known one another casually for some time, actually living together is frequently difficult because there are more intimate interactions and the necessity of sharing time, attention, and space. Children who have been best friends on the playground and after school may suddenly find themselves sharing a room, parental attention, and time in the bathroom, and adults quickly discover that nothing in the household seems familiar. One wants tofu in the refrigerator while others crave meat and potatoes. Where is the good TV going to go—in the bedroom or in the family room? The dog and cat, strangers to each other, fight constantly as they struggle with conflicts over turf. The many interpersonal differences that surface every day can seem inconsequential to outsiders. However, until negotiation of these differences and the passage of time lead to a sense of familiarity, all the family members are likely to feel unappreciated, out of control, and as though they do not belong.

While these feelings may be shared by all family members, particular stressors tend to be associated with being a stepparent, a remarried parent, or a child in a stepfamily household. Because of these differences, each stepfamily member is dealing with personal pain of a slightly different nature, and therefore may find it difficult to empathize with the feelings of the others in the family. One helpful way of increasing understanding between the adults and between adults and children is to call the parent's and stepparent's attention to the basic human needs and the deprivation of them caused initially by external stepfamily structure. Since we all experience rejection, helplessness, and alienation at times during our lives, awareness of and sensitivity to these emotions can serve to increase empathy for others in the family. Children, however, may not be able to empathize with adults until they are of an age when they have gained some emotional independence from their parents and stepparents. Still, they may be able to understand that their *own* feelings are predictable under the circumstances, and this realization can raise their self-esteem.

Reactions of Stepparents

The stepparent has joined an existing alliance of parent and child and comes in as an outsider, a position that is antithetical to the need to belong. In addition, the stepparent routinely is not accepted by stepchildren or by the children's parent in their other household. Often, the newly remarried parent is not able to empathize with the plight of the stepparent, and therefore fails to be supportive. Society also appears to have difficulty dealing with stepparents (Coleman & Ganong, 1987; Fine, 1992b). It is a lonely position, one in which the stepparent may meet active hostility and rejection.

After a discussion with her therapist about these needs and how difficult it is to have them met in stepfamilies before achieving a certain degree of integration, this stepmother responded with much emotion:

> It isn't that you feel uncomfortable for three hours on Monday, are rejected by a colleague at work on Wednesday, and feel as though you don't belong in the group at the party on Saturday. It's all those things at once, each day when you get up and go to breakfast with the kids and their dad, when you hear the phone ring only for your spouse, when you greet your step-

children after school with no response from them, and
spend the evening wishing you'd be welcome to help
with homework or to play a game. You don't go home
to recover from the slights of the world; you feel slight-
ed when you do go home.

It is easy to see why in therapy a stepparent's need for
acceptance, understanding, and support is very great.

Reactions of Remarried Parents

Remarried parents usually have experienced a loss of time
and emotional closeness with their children following the
remarriage and they may also become a target of anger from
the children because of the remarriage. This anger may be
particularly strong when the remarriage follows the death
of a former spouse or a divorce following an affair. As a
result, the remarried parent may fear further loss of important and meaningful relationships with the children and
find it difficult to set limits for them especially when the
remarried parent is the nonresidential parent. They will
often attempt to placate the former spouse in an attempt to
ensure continued contact with the children.

In addition, remarried parents may fear more loss of
relationship with the children if they form a primary
alliance with a new stepparent. This fear of loss of the
children's affections by the remarried parent clashes with
the need of the stepparent to be accepted, to be loved, and
to belong. Commonly, remarried parents in this dilemma
believe themselves to be caught in the middle between
their children and their new partners, and they feel helpless. In actuality, the remarried parent is the most powerful individual in the household because he or she is part of
both the couple subsystem and the parent–child subsystem, with the children and the new partner often
competing for the remarried parent's affection. Being a
loving parent and a loving partner are different roles and
do require the balancing of time and attention, but it is not

an "either one or the other" proposition as many remarried parents seem to feel.

Needs are not right or wrong. They require understanding and acceptance. Therapy can help the adults become aware of these basic needs, have empathy for one another, and find ways to respond to the needs. For example, a remarried parent can thank the partner for things he or she does for the children, kindness for which stepparents tend to get no thanks from their stepchildren; stepparents can support the parent–child relationship when they understand the depth of the parent's fear of loss of the children's love.

Reactions of Children

The children are dealing primarily with feelings of lack of control, and they can also fear loss of relationship with their parents. They usually feel that they have been plucked from their original family and dropped into a totally different family place. They feel out of control and fearful of more loss (Bray, 1992). In reaction they may attempt to gain control in unproductive ways. Their need is for as much control as is possible and appropriate. Their fear of more loss is inextricably related to the way in which their two households respond. Fifty percent of children move between their two households, and when the adults are able to put aside their own fears enough to cooperate because of love for their children, the children's loyalty conflicts and fears of loss of relationships with both of their parents can be significantly reduced. This is a special gift to the children, and also to all the parenting adults since a minimal amount of trust and understanding between households can alleviate the parents' fear of loss and result in children who are happier and easier to be around.

Because of the importance of understanding and helping the children to adjust, Chapter 6 is devoted entirely to this topic.

The Value of Considering Basic Emotional Needs

What is the value of looking at the basic emotional need to belong, to be loved and appreciated, and to have personal power and how do these needs relate to stepfamily dynamics?

(1) Attempting to untangle the dilemmas arising in stepfamilies can be confusing because of the number of individuals involved and the complexity of the stepfamily supra system. These basic needs are a foundation upon which many day-to-day successes or deficiencies are built. Therefore, using them as guidelines can lead to an understanding of what is occurring emotionally in the family. This is helpful for therapists and also for their clients.

Take the lengthy and heated argument between Marjorie and Roland over her insistence that her ancient bathroom scale replace his modern one in the master bathroom. The couple had been married for only a few weeks, and both were finding the adjustment more difficult than they had expected. Marjorie had not been married before. Roland had been married previously and had three grown children who were living on their own. Both adults had been used to living alone, and now Marjorie was moving into the large apartment Roland had lived in since his divorce.

As the therapist explored the situation with the couple, Marjorie talked about the fact that most of her things were in a storage room. She commented, "I opened all the kitchen drawers and there wasn't enough room for any of my utensils. My scale is not nearly as nice as Roland's, but I just want to have something of mine in the house." The therapist understood Marjorie's need to belong and to feel a part of the household, and she was able to empathize with Marjorie and not view her story negatively.

(2) The therapist asked Marjorie if perhaps she was feeling as though she did not belong in the house and if the use of her scale was a way of attempting to feel more connected. At this point, Marjorie began to cry. She felt accepted and understood by her therapist, and the question had clarified for her why she had been behaving in this

way. Then she began to talk at some length about her sense of alienation. Roland listened quietly.

(3) Using this basic concept, the therapist was able to help the couple understand each other's actions and respond to each other with empathy. Roland could now identify with the feelings Marjorie was having, and the need to argue the matter disappeared.

(4) After a few minutes, with the situation clarified, Roland and Marjorie discussed moving some of Marjorie's furniture into the apartment to replace some of Roland's things. They also began to explore other ways of helping Marjorie feel a part of her new surroundings.

To summarize, using the concept of basic human needs as a foundation:

- Many day-to-day stepfamily situations become clear and this simplification leads to understanding.
- With this understanding, the therapist is more likely to feel empathy for stepfamily members; as a result, the therapy is more effective.
- Stepfamily individuals can use these perceptions to understand and empathize with each other.
- Understanding and empathy enables stepfamily members to find ways to help meet each other's important emotional needs.

The task has become one of acceptance and caring, inclusion in the day-to-day family activities, and the creation of a family identity to provide familiar structure and predictability. The path to familiarity, to feelings of belonging, and to being in control is built not only by the passage of time but also by communication and negotiation, creativity and inclusiveness. Familiarity develops from the combining of past approaches and experiences to meet a variety of needs, as well as from the development of satisfying new rituals negotiated by the family unit. Often stepfamilies need therapeutic intervention to help them gain this empathy for and understanding of the feelings of other family members and to assist them in working out ways of accomplishing all the tasks that arise for this type of family. Therapists are finding that short-term therapeutic measures appear to be all that is needed with about two-thirds of stepfamilies who come for help with their process of integration. With the remaining one-third, because their difficulties impinge on a sensitive and painful area for one or more family members, a longer, move involved therapeutic process is usually required to help them make needed changes and accept and value what they have accomplished.

EMOTIONAL STAGES IN STEPFAMILY INTEGRATION

In her book, *Becoming a Stepfamily*, Papernow (1993) explores in detail the emotional stages experienced by stepfamily members as they accomplish the necessary tasks and move towards family identity and integration. Basic to Papernow's seven stages are the following important steps on the road that leads to stepfamily progress:

1. From the stepparent's feelings of isolation and rejection to acceptance and belonging;
2. From the remarried parent's fear of loss to security in the parent–child relationship;
3. From the children's experience of loss and lack of control to an appreciation of the new;
4. From tenseness and apprehension of all family members to the relaxation that comes from living in a rewarding, familiar, and predictable environment.

Being made aware of these and Papernow's predictable stages is comforting for remarriage family members caught in a whirlwind of stepfamily emotions because these stages normalize their experience and render it much less personal. It also increases their self-esteem and thus increases their ability to deal with the events occurring in the family. For us, the validity of these stages is demonstrated by stepfamily members who express great relief when they recognize themselves and their particular stage of development in the family. With this recognition many then look ahead to making further emotional progress. Following is a description of the seven stages proposed by Papernow (1993):

1. *Fantasy.* Initially most adults expect their new stepfamily to settle down quickly and begin to function smoothly soon after they come together. This fantasy stage tends to be short-lived once the individuals move together under one roof.

2. *Immersion.* This represents a stage in which family members feel "immersed" in rough waters rather than floating on calm seas. Unfamiliar and unanticipated situations seem to arise every few minutes, and discomfort and tension are continually just below the surface of the family interactions.

3. *Awareness.* There is a growing awareness that some changes are needed. As a rule, the stepparents are feeling like outsiders and begin to push for an alliance with their partners. The remarried parents feel caught in the middle, pulled in two directions by their spouses and by their children. In tense times, the family splits along biological lines. It often takes some type of external validation for stepparents before they trust their feelings and begin to insist on changes.

4. *Mobilization.* This is the stage at which couples often come for therapy. Strong emotions have surfaced, and there are many arguments. The family continues to split along biological lines when there is friction. From our perspective, there is a clash between the human needs just discussed—the stepparents' "need to be accepted, to be appreciated, and to belong; the remarried parents'...fear of loss of closeness with their chil-

dren; and the children's need to retain the close relationship with their parents."

5. *Action.* On the average it takes three to four years to reach this important stage where the adult couple begins to form a solid alliance and works as a team to meet the family challenges. The parent and stepparent have realized that the children need the stability of a strong couple and the model of adults who can work together, and the remarried parent is able to support the stepparent in interactions with his or her stepchildren. In turn, the stepparent is supportive of the relationship between the parent and the children. A necessary boundary around the couple is developed and at the same time the couple respects and responds to the needs of the children.

6. *Contact.* As the household reaches this stage, the step relationships are beginning to develop and grow to the point where stepparents become "intimate outsiders" (Papernow, 1993), and everyone enjoys the sense of control and predictability that comes from the now familiar patterns of stepfamily life.

7. *Resolution.* There is now a security in the household, and for many stepfamilies cooperation takes place between the children's two homes. At special family times such as graduations, weddings, births, and deaths, the family may experience disruption as in earlier stages, but the group works this through more amicably and more quickly than would have been initially possible. Even when the family has reached this stage, research indicates that successful stepfamilies continue to be less cohesive and more flexible than first-marriage families (Hetherington, Stanley-Hagan, & Anderson, 1989).

Stepfamily members' self-esteem is high as they begin to find satisfaction in their ability to deal with stepfamily situations, and they experience the satisfactions provided by the richer, more complex, and diverse stepfamily "supra system" described by Sager et al. (1983). They often express this by saying things like, "Because of my stepfamily experience I have the feeling that I will be able to deal with whatever situations life gives me."

For further information about these emotional stages, please see Papernow's book listed in the Resources section.

FAMILY RELATIONSHIPS AT DIFFERENT STAGES

Diagrams A, B, and C in Exhibit 2.2 are helpful ways of representing the changes in relationships in the household, with the thickness of the lines representing the positive strength of the various relationships. While they are simplified and give an idealistic picture of a nuclear family, new stepfamily, and an integrated stepfamily, we have found these diagrams to be of great value to many stepfamily members. Drawing similar diagrams to reflect the individuals in a particular family can be very revealing to that family. In addition, by relating the relationship patterns depicted to feelings of alienation or outsider status and of not being recognized or appreciated, family members frequently feel understood and validated. This helps to create a therapeutic alliance with the family. Family members may also be more able to identify with and accept the emotions of others in the family.

CONCLUSION

Feelings and behavior are the basic building blocks of our day-to-day existence. Indeed, the interaction of these major components of our personal experience influence our relationships with others and is an important determinant of the interpersonal environment in any family. While the foregoing descriptions have separated feelings

Exhibit 2.2. Changes in Family Relationships.

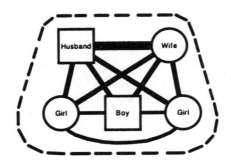

A. Nuclear Family

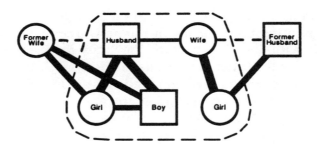

B. New Stepfamily

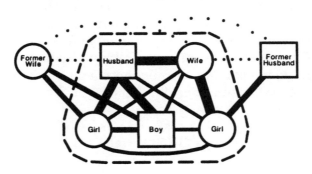

C. Integrated Stepfamily

Reprinted from Visher & Visher, (1988), *Old Loyalties, New Ties: Therapeutic Strategies with Stepfamilies,* New York: Brunner/ Mazel. p. 13.

and behavior, in reality they are intimately connected. The outlines help distinguish stepfamily norms in each of these two parts of our consciousness, and can act as therapeutic guides regardless of one's theoretical approach.

Often stepfamilies come for therapy with no sense of stepfamily norms. It is important for therapists to be familiar with stepfamily structure, the resultant tasks, the basic emotional needs involved, and the predictable emotional stages. Without this foundation, both the family and the therapist may attempt to proceed using original family norms as the model. This approach can lead to family disintegration rather than to stepfamily integration. These basic building blocks provide the foundation for the information given in the following chapters.

3

WORKING WITH STEPFAMILY DIFFERENCES

This chapter looks at 16 basic differences between step-family life and first marriage and calls attention to the therapeutic implications inherent in each of these aspects. Table 3.1 lists these 16 characteristics and their therapeutic implications, and it serves as the outline for this chapter.

BASIC STEPFAMILY DIFFERENCES

1. There Are Different Structural Characteristics.

The seven structural characteristics are discussed at some length in Chapter 2. Because of these differences, the idealized nuclear family model is not appropriate for remarriage families, and it is imperative that we carry an accurate stepfamily model in our heads so that we do not misjudge stepfamily individuals. Stepfamilies must be evaluated with the use of appropriate stepfamily norms. For example, a lack of emotional closeness between a stepparent and a stepchild does not necessarily mean that their family is dysfunctional. Often, it simply calls attention to the fact that the family has not been together long

Table 3.1

**Differences Between Stepfamilies and Nuclear Families
and the Therapeutic Implications**

HOW STEPFAMILIES DIFFER FROM NUCLEAR FAMILIES	THERAPEUTIC IMPLICATIONS
1. There are different structural characteristics.	1. Must evaluate the family using stepfamily norms. A nuclear family model is not valid.
2. There is little or no family loyalty.	2. Initially, seeing the family members together may be unproductive.
3. Prior to integration the family reacts to transitional stresses.	3. The first focus needs to be on the transitional adjustment process, not on intrapsychic processes.
4. Society compares stepfamilies negatively to nuclear families.	4. There is a basic need for acceptance and validation as a worthwhile family unit.
5. There is a long integration period with predictable stages.	5. The stage of family development is very important in the assessment of whom to see in therapy.
6. There is not a breakdown of family homeostasis; equilibrium has never been established.	6. With normalization and education, stability can emerge from chaos and ignorance of the norms.
7. There is a complicated "supra family system."	7. The complications of the family need to be kept in mind during therapy. Drawing a genogram helps.
8. There have been many losses for all individuals.	8. Grief work may be necessary.
9. There are preexisting parent–child coalitions.	9. Developing a secure couple relationship is essential. Many times, "permission" is needed to do this.
10. A solid couple relationship does not signify good stepparent–stepchild relationships.	10. Step relationships take special attention separate from the couple relationship.

(Continued on next page)

(Table 3.1 Continued)

HOW STEPFAMILIES DIFFER FROM NUCLEAR FAMILIES	THERAPEUTIC IMPLICATIONS
11. There is a different balance of power.	11. Stepparents have very little authority in the family initially. Therefore, discipline issues need to be handled by the biological parent. Children have more power, which needs to be channeled positively.
12. There is less family control because there is an influential parent elsewhere or in memory.	12. Appropriate control can be fostered to lessen the anxiety engendered by helplessness.
13. Children have more than two parenting figures.	13. There is a need to think in terms of a "parenting coalition," not a parenting couple.
14. There are ambiguous family boundaries with little agreement as to family history.	14. These losses and stresses may require attention.
15. Initially there is no family history.	15. Members need to share their past histories and develop family rituals and ways of doing things.
16. The emotional climate is intense and unexpected.	16. Empathy with other family members can be encouraged by understanding the human needs that are not being met: to be loved and appreciated, to belong, and to have control over one's life.

enough for individuals to know one another or to have shared the positive memories that are the building blocks of warm interpersonal relationships.

In remarriage families, there can be a diversity and creativity not generally found in first-marriage families, as stepfamilies work out ways to accomplish all the tasks that lead to satisfactory family integration. For example, in the Bennett household, Maria eats dinner with the younger children at 5:30 p.m. and Brian cooks and eats with the older children at 8:30 p.m. after their soccer practice. They all have a meal together on Sundays. The Castles celebrate Christmas on New Year's Eve because that is when the family unit is together; in the Harrison household, Debbie spends one weekend a month with her 15-year-old son who is in a military boarding school and cannot handle the changes in his family life if he goes home on those weekends.

These are not abnormal patterns. The functioning of each of these families needs to be evaluated according to stepfamily norms. The question is the same as with any type of family: Is the family moving towards more solid interpersonal relationships, increased satisfaction, and personal growth?

2. There Is Little or No Family Loyalty.

It takes a feeling of familiarity for individuals to feel comfortable in a group and to develop a sense of loyalty to the group, and it takes time for a sense of belonging to develop. Initially, in remarriage families, everything tends to feel unfamiliar for everyone. There is a new person or new people coming together with others with different ways of doing things, from turning on the television to cooking the hamburgers. At first, tension can easily split the household along biological lines. Until the couple has had time to learn to work together as a team, seeing the children and adults together in therapy can split the group even more widely apart. With little or no loyalty to the new family unit the children may be upset and make very hurtful comments that pit the adults against one another. As one stepmother described the early days with her husband and his children, "I felt as though I were walking on eggshells. Things felt very fragile." Family members may need to talk about their very strong feelings, but without the bonding that can take place over time, it may be advisable to speak separately with the adults and with the subgroups of children who have some commitment to one another.

3. Prior to Integration the Family Is Reacting to Transitional Stresses.

Transitions of any kind can be upsetting. The lack of stability during these periods often results in feelings of anxiety and loss of control. As the new situation becomes more familiar and predictable, anxiety usually subsides.

Stepfamily members are moving from single-parent households towards an integrated remarriage household. It is similar to the acculturation process that occurs when a family emigrates from one culture to another, and viewing it in this perspective is often helpful to some families.

Judith Landau-Stanton (1985) has worked with many emigrating families, and she believes, as we do, that transitional stresses can produce psychological symptoms in stepfamilies just as they do in families attempting to adapt to a new cultural pattern. We also agree with Landau-Stanton, Griffiths, and Mason (1982) that, "The conflicts arising from transitional factors must provide the initial focus for therapy" (p. 368). In some stepfamilies, there may be personal problems that will require simultaneous attention, but in our opinion the primary focus of therapy needs to be on the transitional adjustment process rather than on intrapsychic processes. Perhaps this new stepmother was reacting to the need for this type of therapeutic approach when she was feeling upset about her therapy and said, "He (the therapist) wouldn't allow me to talk about being a stepmother. He said I was becoming obsessed with the role." A new stepmother certainly can bring insecurities and unrealistic expectations with her into her new role, but dealing with these issues tends to be unproductive if she is being treated disrespectfully by her stepchildren or is not being supported in the family by her husband. Therapy first needs to address these all too common interpersonal transitional stresses.

4. Society Compares Stepfamilies Negatively to Nuclear Families.

When first-marriage families come for therapy, they may not be receiving the support they need from society, but they do have acceptance that theirs is an important and valuable family form. Stepfamilies do not receive this favorable affirmation. The presence of a stepparent dims society's rosy glow attitude toward the family unit. College students put stepfamilies at the bottom of the list when asked to rank different types of families (Coleman & Ganong, 1987). This example illustrates the generally negative environment for remarriage families and therefore their special need for acceptance and validation.

It is important to feel that your family is an acceptable family. Yet, because of the negative stereotyping, many stepfamily adults who enter therapy do not reveal that theirs is this type of family. With acceptance and sensitivity, therapists can provide the family with an important antidote to the criticisms of society. No wonder validation of the viability and value of these more complex families was stated to be an essential ingredient of effective stepfamily therapy!

5. There Is a Long Integration Period with Predictable Stages.

Earlier, in Chapter 2, we outlined the seven stages of emotional development Papernow (1993) has studied, and we mentioned not bringing children and adults together until there has been time for some family loyalty to develop. The experiential stage of the family is closely related to the development of relationships and we see the assessment of the emotional stage that the family has reached as an important consideration in deciding whom to see together in family therapy. This is an extremely important assessment and Table 3.2 provides suggestions for the different subgroups we believe can work productively together at each developmental stage of the family. Following the table is a more detailed description of our ideas.

At first, the parent–child bonds may be stronger than the bond between the new couple. Until the Action Stage where the two adults have learned to work together as a team, it can be divisive rather than integrative to see the children and the adults together during the same session. Under stress, the family continues to split along biological lines until this stage, and even in a therapeutic setting this can lead to negative interchanges that cannot be satisfactorily reframed or retracted. In sharing these ideas with therapists, a number of practitioners have spoken about disastrous initial interviews, even when the intent was simply to observe the interactions in the family. Not seeing the household unit even for an evaluation can make several valuable contributions:

a. It may be the first time the couple has ever had the opportunity to work on a family situation alone, without the presence of the children. This helps to support and strengthen the new couple relationship.

b. The therapist may get more, rather than less, information about family functioning. This is because the adults are freer to talk about their feelings and perceptions when the children are not present. If the children are seen without the adults, they also have more freedom to say what they would like to say.

c. The therapist is more in control. With the volatility of many remarriage families this can be important.

As can be seen in Table 3.2, when the stage is reached in which the couple is working relatively well together, a

Table 3.2

Stages of Emotional Development *

Stage	Characteristics	Whom to See
Fantasy	Adults expect instant love and adjustment. Children try to ignore stepparent in the hope that he/she will go away and biological parents will be reunited.	Individual; Couple; Stepfamily household (unlikely to see anyone except for education).
Immersion	Attempts to realize fantasies. Vague sense that things are not going well. Increasing negativity. Splits along biological lines. Stepparent feels something is wrong with him/her.	Individual; Couple; Older children if disturbed.
Awareness	Growing awareness of family pressures. Stepparent begins to perceive what changes are needed. Parent feels pulled between needs of children and of new spouse. Groups divide along biological lines. Children may observe and exploit differences between couple.	Couple seen individually and/or conjointly; Children seen if they need help.
Mobilization	Strong emotions begin to be expressed, often leading to arguments between couple. Stepparent clear on need for change. Parent fears change will bring loss. Sharp division between biological groups. Stepparent with no children is in isolated position and lacks support.	Couple seen individually and/or conjointly; Children seen if they need help.
Action	Couple begins working together in attempts to find solutions. Family structure changes. Boundaries are clarified. Children may resist changes.	Emphasis on couple; Appropriate subgroups; Suprasystem subgroup combinations.
Contact	Couple working well together. Closer bonding between stepparent and stepchild and other steprelations. Stepparent has definite role with stepchildren. Boundaries clear. More ability to deal with suprasystem issues.	Any suprasystem grouping (depends on issues).
Resolution	Stepfamily identity secure. When difficulties arise family may regress to earlier stages, but moves ahead quickly. Usual difficulties are around nodal family events involving the suprasystem.	Any suprasystem grouping (unlikely to come in now).

* Adapted from Papernow (1993). *Becoming a Stepfamily: Patterns of Development in Remarried Families.* San Francisco: Jossey-Bass.

number of subgroups can be combined in one session. Of course, it is often valuable to see individuals and subgroups or the total unit in different combinations, i.e., two adults together and individually, or the couple and two subgroups of children at different times, or one large group of all the adults and children.

When one considers the emotional intensity of stepfamilies, the use of more than one therapist can be very helpful. In one instance, a therapist with little stepfamily experience asked a therapist who was a stepmother to work with her when seeing the whole stepfamily unit. Together, the two therapists formed a strong and informed therapy team, and the family made considerable progress.

The following are important suggestions for therapists when seeing subgroups together, particularly when they include individuals from both of the children's households:

a. Make appointments directly with any adult you wish to see. Do not send messages through individuals you may already be seeing.
b. Do not call the other household until you have permission from the adults you are already seeing.
c. When seeing individuals from the "other" household, let them know that their perceptions and concerns are important to you in your attempts to help the children they all share.
d. Be sure there is mutual agreement about the fees and who will pay them. In nearly all instances, families respond well to paying for *their* sessions because they are coming to be helpful to their children who have two households where they belong and where adults care about their welfare. When you are seeing individuals from more than one household, suggest that each couple pay an equal share for each session. For example, if one couple offers to pay the total amount for the session, it is best not to accept this offer as this gives the message that the therapy hour is for the

couple that is paying rather than in the interest of the children they all care about. If each pays half, it is because the adults in both households care about their shared child and are sharing the costs of therapy.

e. See each couple alone at least once to be sure the two are working together satisfactorily. This also gives them the opportunity to express any negative feelings they may have about the children's "other household."

f. Keep the joint sessions focused on the issue of the child. It is almost never productive to attempt to resolve old hurts; the meeting is to deal with a current situation involving the children and their two households.

Patricia Papernow's (1993) study of the stages that stepfamily members experience during the process of family integration indicates that this process takes a great deal longer than most stepfamily adults expect. Having a realistic idea of the average length of time it takes stepfamilies to feel integrated allows some adults to relax and not feel that there is something wrong with them or with their family.

While there are "slow" families and "fast" families, it generally takes about 4–5 years for the stepfamily integration process to reach a satisfactory level. With younger children the process tends to take a shorter time; on the other hand, with teenagers in a new stepfamily, there may never be enough time for the family to solidify relationships before the adolescents are living on their own. Later on, as independent young adults, they often form adult, rather than parent–child, relationships with parents and stepparents.

Stepfamily integration is an area in which additional reading could be helpful. *Becoming a Stepfamily: Patterns of Development in Remarried Families* by Patricia Papernow is the basic source for learning about the stages in stepfamily formation in detail.

Chapter 4 in our book, *Old Loyalties, New Ties: Thera-peutic Strategies with Stepfamilies*, is devoted to "Whom to See Therapy." There are also helpful suggestions in the chapter by Browning listed in "References for Therapists and Counselors" in the Resources section.

6. There Is Not a Breakdown of Family Homeostasis; Equilibrium Has Never Been Established.

When individuals or nuclear families seek therapy, as a rule some event or situation has upset the equilibrium of the household. The therapeutic task becomes one of help-ing the individuals or family members to change in ways that are necessary for the family to regain satisfactory stability. In contrast, stepfamily members typically come to therapy because they do not know how to establish stability and necessary family balance. For these families, psychoeducation and normalization of stepfamily life is often a key to their ability to work out a satisfactory homeostasis, as the Hector Family illustrates:

Mary and Jim Hector had been living together for one year before being married six months ago. The year had been stressful for them, but they had ex-pected that the children would be less stressed after the adults were married. However, this had not hap-pened. Jim's three children and Mary's two children were more upset than ever. The two youngest stepsiblings were girls, and these were the two the couple worried about the most. Mary's daughter Martha and Jim's daughter Jenny were fighting con-stantly. Although both of them were eight years old, they were very dissimilar. For example, Jenny was outgoing and outspoken, while Martha was quiet and eager to please.

In talking with the couple the therapist felt she had begun to see the probable cause of the girls' friction. Jim liked his daughter Jenny's high energy and ex-cused her frequently hurtful remarks by saying she was only eight and not old enough to understand her impact on others. He disliked Martha's "shyness" as he called it, and kept pushing her to be more like Jenny. Martha's mother Mary had begun to view her daughter's behavior negatively in the same way her husband did and began to criticize Martha for not "speaking up." Martha's special ability to get along well with people and make many positive contributions to the family was being overlooked. As the therapist viewed it, Martha was feeling increasingly upset, insecure, and angry at Jenny, whom she saw receiving the adults' approval.

The constant friction between the two girls was leading to arguments between Mary and Jim, and even the older children in the family were negatively affected and complained that the younger two were getting all the attention. The emotional tension in the household seldom disappeared and the family unit had not yet managed to work out a predictable and satisfying way of functioning together.

This family needed to know more about what to expect in this type of family, and they needed the support that can come from a therapist who can normalize their experience for them. In this case their therapist helped the adults understand the many changes and losses for all the children and each one's need for special one-on-one time with his or her parent to maintain that important exclusive connection, as well as time with the stepparent to begin to form a caring relationship with this new person.

The couple also began to understand that they were dealing with family differences in an all-too-common way by expecting two children with different biological heredity and different family-of-origin experiences to be alike. In such instances, one child often becomes the "model" and the other one is judged negatively.

Jim and Mary began to relate more warmly to all the children and to see the "specialness" of each of the eight-year-olds. Then Martha and Jenny started to get along better, and as Mary and Jim's expectations became more realistic, they relaxed and the family began to function more and more effectively.

Because stepfamilies are attempting to solidify and integrate rather than undo some changes that have disturbed the family's equilibrium, the number of family sessions may be fewer than with upset nuclear families.

7. There Is a Complicated "Supra Family System."

Sager et al. (1983) refer to a remarriage family's "supra family system." Unlike original families, there are former spouses and former in-laws and marriage relationships. As a result there is a complexity of relationships that often go unrecognized by stepfamily members. Drawing a family genogram can serve many important functions, two major ones being:

1. To illustrate why living in a stepfamily can feel overwhelming at times
2. To give family members (and those working with them) a sense of more control

Having the supra family system represented graphically can make it appear clear and manageable for many individuals.

We consider that "family therapy" does not mean gathering everyone together in the office. It does mean having a concept of the total family and their interrelationships in mind when working with different family members. In the case of stepfamilies, this family picture will be more complex than for other types of families and can extend across several households. In stepfamily genograms, it can be helpful to indicate the amount of time children spend in each of two households. This can be done by using dots for short time periods up to a solid line for full time, as indicated in Exhibit 4.1 on p. 72.

8. There Have Been Many Losses for All Individuals.

Change brings loss, even when it is a welcome change, and marriage brings with it many changes. Remarriage, however, involves important losses not present in original marriages, such as the loss of full-time parent–child relationships, the loss of marriage dreams and fantasies, and the loss of familiar surroundings for everyone. Throughout this book, the subject of loss is frequently mentioned because it is such an important element in remarriage. When one is treating stepfamilies, there may be a need to deal with the sadness and grief that have an importance not commonly seen in first-marriage families.

9. There Are Preexisting Parent–Child Alliances.

In a stepfamily, one or both of the adults have a child from a previous relationship. The new couple comes together with the existence of prior parent–child alliances, and the strength of those relationships can vary widely and affect the couple relationship in many ways.

Many parents who remarry have difficulty forming a new couple relationship because they fear that to do so is betraying the earlier parent–child relationship. However, as in any family, it takes a solid couple to create a well-functioning family, so that developing a secure couple relationship may be the most important therapeutic task. At times, it seems as though the "permission" of the therapist is needed for a parent to form a new relationship.

While successful stepfamilies need to be headed by a well-functioning couple, the parent–child alliances may remain stronger in these families than in those found in well-functioning nuclear families (White & Booth, 1985). If, however, the parent–child coalition remains very strong and the couple relationship remains distant, the new partner will often then resent the stepchild. In contrast, a solid couple relationship can provide a family climate in which important parent–child relationships are not threatening to the new partner, and in which stepparent–stepchild relationships can grow. As the respondents to the Therapy Research Questionnaire indicated, forming a strong couple bond was crucial for the family and was one of the most important aspects of their therapy experience.

10. A Solid Couple Relationship Does Not Signify Good Stepparent–Stepchild Relationships.

In first-marriage families, when the parents work well together and have a solid relationship, the parent–child relationships in the family tend to be good ones. However, this is not found to be the case in stepfamilies (Crosbie-Burnett, 1984). Often, stepfamily couples separate, even though they have a warm and rewarding couple relationship, because stepparent–stepchild bonding has not developed. These step relationships may need special attention separate from the couple relationship. However, a good couple relationship generally must precede the forming of satisfactory stepparent–stepchild relationships. Without this solid couple relationship, stepparents are likely to compete with their stepchildren for the attention of their spouse.

Remarried parents often push for good relationships between their children and their new partner, and sometimes therapists are in the position of seeing the stepparent–stepchild dyad to help improve that relationship. The couple may have a positive bond between them and seeing the stepparent and stepchild together may be indicated. In such instances, the balance within the household needs to be kept in mind.

In one instance, Denise pushed for her husband, Terence, to work on his relationship with her teenage son, Donald. Denise and Terence had reached the place in therapy where they were working well together in the family;

however, Donald was still resisting the changes and running away from time to time. Terence and Donald were seen together by the therapist and their relationship improved greatly. However, Denise at this point sabotaged the situation and no one was willing to continue in therapy. It seems likely that Denise wanted Terence and Donald to have a good relationship but had not realized that it meant sharing her son with another adult. She had lived alone with Donald for three years before her remarriage, and the therapist may have needed to include her in the therapy with her new husband and her son so that she would also be involved with the changes. The therapist would also have the opportunity to become aware of the complex interactions taking place.

In another stepfamily, the couple was still working on their relationship when the wife, Ann, came to their appointment saying that she was feeling totally left out at home. As she put it, "I might as well not be around. I don't feel needed because Greg (her new husband) and my kids have a great time together and they don't need me."

Greg responded by saying, "Yeah. I see what Ann means. I pushed for the kids to do things with me and I stuck up for them with their mother sometimes. Even when I told them what to do they allowed me to do that. Ann *is* being left out. I guess I should have consulted with her."

Even though remarried parents want these step relationships to develop, this is not an easy change for them. They are sensitive to shifts in their relationships with their children, and need therapeutic support and understanding.

11. There Is a Different Balance of Power.

In original families, the balance of power in functional families lies with the couple. In stepfamilies, stepparents enter with very little authority as far as the children are concerned. The power in the household rests with the parent of the children. When a stepparent has no children in the household, this nonauthoritative position can be very difficult to handle. If the stepparent is married to a parent whose children live elsewhere most of the time, this stepparent is in the least powerful position of all the adults as far as the children are concerned, and may find it difficult to deal with the strong sense of helplessness he or she experiences.

One way to help stepparents is to encourage them to find areas outside the family that bring them satisfaction. At times, when they marry and form a stepfamily, stepmothers plan to leave satisfying work situations in order to "take care of the children." It may be important for them to remain working outside the home because they may need the external support and acceptance of others to help balance the lack of authority within the new household. Helping them to at least delay the decision to leave their outside work until they have a better chance to experience the stepfamily can give them the opportunity to better assess their situation.

Stepfamily research is finding that teenagers in new stepfamilies have more power than they do in nuclear families (Bray, 1992). Often, they have been given more adult privileges and responsibilities during the single-parent household phase and when the remarriage takes place they usually do not care to return to a less adult status. The adults frequently need help in understanding the importance of allowing their adolescents to continue to have considerable control over their own lives so that they use their power in the family in constructive rather than in destructive ways.

It usually takes months or even years for stepparents of all but very young children to work their way into a co-management role with the remarried parent. From the first, the couple needs to work together on how the two wish the family to operate, but initially it is the parent of the children who has the authority to implement the decisions. The older the children, the more important it is to solicit their input into family decisions. Productive family meetings are helpful in any family; they are especially valuable in stepfamilies. However, it may take the experience of family meetings in the therapist's office to enable the family to work together at home.

The issue of power is an area of difficulty in many stepfamilies, and examples of therapeutic interchanges are given in Section 7 of Chapter 4.

12. There Is Less Family Control Because There Is an Influential Parent Elsewhere or in Memory.

The basic psychological need for control over one's life is not as well met in remarriage families as it is in first-marriage families. In stepfamilies, there is a parent living elsewhere or remaining within the children's minds and hearts if the parent has died. This person exerts an influence on the household through the children because the biological parent is always important to the children. Because of this, in many stepfamily households the adults feel helpless and become angry or discouraged and depressed.

Since feeling helpless is very upsetting, it is not surprising that many stepfamily adults who have been in therapy cite a reduction in their sense of helplessness as one of the most positive aspects of their therapy experience. This indicates that therapists often need to help remarried parents and stepparents deal creatively and satisfactorily with the decreased autonomy characteristic of remarriage families.

Two common reactions stepfamily adults have in response to diminished control are:

   a. The adults in one household attempt to control the individuals in the other household.
   b. The adults relinquish the control they do have and therefore become more helpless than is actually necessary.

The first reaction reflects a usual response to interpersonal difficulties—if only the other person would change, everything would work out! Helping the adults recognize that they cannot control the other household can become an important therapeutic task. The second reaction is related to the first in that the adults are failing to realize that they, in turn, cannot be controlled by the children's other household. Frequently, they have been so caught in anger at the adults in the other household that they don't take steps to reduce their frustration in ways that they can control. Indeed, a number of remarried parents attempt to gain some control by seeking legal help and resorting to the courts as a way to deal with their sense of helplessness. Others may expect the therapist to exert influence on the other household.

Tim Ryan is an example of a remarried father who became involved in a power struggle with his former wife over seeing his two children. He sought both legal and psychological help, spending large sums on each over a two-year period. His therapist was understanding and clear with him about his boundaries and what control he did have. The therapist also explored with him the antecedents of his tendency to get into power struggles with a number of different people. His growing years had been unhappy ones under the tutelage of a stern and dictatorial mother, and his reaction to this had been to become self-sufficient at age 19 and to resist situations in which he felt constrained by others.

Tim's therapist also referred him to a stepfamily support group. With their help and the support of his therapist, Tim was able to drop his legal fight to have more "visiting rights" with his children. He let the children know he would always welcome times with them, and he stopped pressuring his former wife, who had sole physical custody of the children. Not only did he begin to enjoy his friends and activities more without this continuous struggle, but his former wife found that it benefited her to have the children with their father at times. She decided she would like more time for her own social life, and she discovered that having the children with their father more often worked very well for her. Tim was quick to see the advantages of avoiding unnecessary power struggles.

More frequently, stepfamily struggles are concerned with such things as parents not coming for their children at the agreed time, not returning the children when expected, or allowing them to eat candy between meals or stay up late at night. In Marcia and Robert's case their therapist helped them order their own lives so that they would not be personally affected if Marcia's former husband did not come for the children on time. When they had plans to go out, they left as planned and arranged for a neighborhood teenager to stay with the 11-year-old twins until their father came for them. "Letting go" of the struggle in these situations is not easy, but can be encouraged. Finding solutions to situations such as the one in which Marcia and Robert found themselves, parents and stepparents learn to take control where they can and to respond with more understanding and acceptance of the limitations imposed on them by their more complex type of family.

13. Children Have More Than Two Parenting Figures.

In the past, children were often raised by more than two parents in large, extended families. However, society in this country and in similar cultures appears to have developed great difficulty thinking in terms of children having more than two parenting figures in their lives. This is reflected in the fact that stepparents are not legally or socially acknowledged as parental figures, and divorced parents at times take the position that "no other woman (man) is going to tell my children what they can do." Even in non-stepfamily disputes over parenting rights, there are numerous reports of judges cutting children off from adults who care about them by awarding custody of the children to biological parents rather than to adoptive or stepparents. Often, custody is awarded to adults the children have never known rather than to the adults who have raised them.

There are signs that there may be some changes in these patterns. Several years ago, a newspaper reported that a judge in Massachusetts allowed a stepfather to adopt his stepchild, while the child's father had visiting rights. The advent of "open adoptions" leads in the same direction. This trend towards more openness is acknowledging that children can have emotional ties to more than two parent figures. Even though some of these connections may disappear over the years, it seems emotionally advantageous for both the children and the adults not to require a sudden cutoff of relationships where positive relationships exist. It is important for therapists to conceptualize that children often have three or four parenting figures. Indeed, children may retain ties to former stepparents after a divorce or death of their remarried parent. The legal system and many of our institutions continue to operate as though the original two parents are the only adults involved with children, even when the children have one or two stepparents in their lives. On the other hand, therapists often think only in terms of the adult couple with whom they are working and fail to include the parent in the children's other household, and the new partner if that person is remarried or in a long-term relationship. Both views omit adults who can be important to the children.

It is helpful for children if their parents have formed a co-parenting relationship after a divorce (Wallerstein & Kelly, 1980). After a remarriage, clinical observation suggests that children benefit greatly when parents and stepparents can work together across the households as a "parenting coalition" (Visher & Visher, 1988; 1989). This cooperation can also reduce the hostility between the adults, so that everyone benefits, adults as well as children.

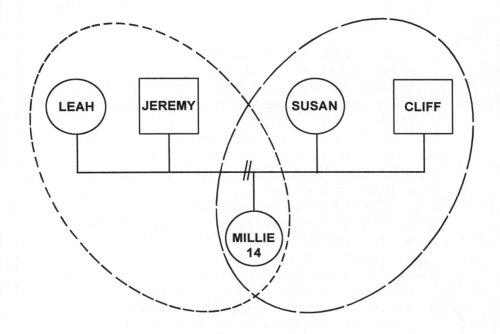

Exhibit 3.1. Millie's two families.

In the case of Susan and Cliff and Leah and Jeremy (Exhibit 3.1), the ability to form a "parenting coalition" not only changed 14-year-old Millie's life, it also reduced to a great extent the emotional burden felt by the adults.

In a post-divorce scenario typical of many separating couples, Millie's parents, Susan and Jeremy, continued to fight with each other about money, living arrangements, and the raising of Millie, who was 8 at the time her parents divorced. A few years later, both parents had remarried, and the bickering continued, at times flaring into heated arguments on the telephone.

Eventually, Millie was referred for therapy by her school counsellor. She was now 14 and was quite withdrawn. She was not doing well academically and did not have friends at school.

The therapist saw Millie for several months and, although she seemed to be happier, it was clear to her therapist that the hostility between her two households was continuing and was of great concern to Millie.

Millie lived most of the time with her mother, Susan, and her stepfather, Cliff, and saw her father, Jeremy, and his wife, Leah, on an irregular basis once or twice a month.

With Millie's permission, Millie's therapist telephoned Susan and Cliff and made an appointment to see them, and she also contacted Jeremy and Leah for an appointment.

Both couples complained about the arguments that took place between Susan and Jeremy, and each couple was given the opportunity to make negative comments about the other household if they wished. The therapist supported their caring for Millie and the difficulty of sharing children.

The two couples were warm and caring within their relationship, but were upset across the two households. Among other things, Susan and Cliff felt that Jeremy and Leah were remiss in not having Millie with them more frequently, and Jeremy and Leah felt that Susan and Cliff were trying to control them by wanting to make a definite schedule for having Millie with them. When the therapist suggested they all come together to work out Millie's time between households, Jeremy was reluctant:

Jeremy: Wouldn't that be kissing up to Susan to plan with her and Cliff?

Therapist: Perhaps you could explain to me what you are thinking when you put it that way.

Jeremy: We don't want to be dependent on Susan and Cliff. I don't want them telling me when I can see my own daughter.

Therapist: So, if you are not fighting, it seems as

though you are not in control, is that what you
are saying?

Jeremy: Yes, that's right.

Therapist: And it's working well this way?

Couple, agreeing: No, it isn't, and it does worry
us that Millie seems very sad a lot of the time.

Therapist: Um, so you would like to do something to help Millie.

The four adults and Millie all came together to work
out the contacts for Millie between her two households. Several important interactions took place in
the first joint session:

- Millie asked to come to talk with her therapist
  alone before the joint session. During this period
  she voiced her distress about them all being
  together, and her therapist was able to reduce her
  anxiety.
- Millie slowly relaxed during the joint session
  when she saw the adults all being civil to one
  another.
- At one point near the beginning of the session,
  Jeremy and Susan began to trade negative comments with one another. The therapist inter-
  vened, and reduced the tension by commenting
  on their lack of practice at working out these
  difficult situations. She also complimented them
  for their willingness to come together because of
  their love for Millie.
- At another point later on, Susan said to Leah, "I
  don't envy you your position with Millie. I think
  being a stepmother is the hardest role there is!"

This comment of Susan's was the catalyst for a
thoughtful discussion about the advantage for everyone of planning ahead, but remaining open to negoti-
ating changes in the plans if necessary. It took two
more sessions during the next month, with input from

the adults and also from Millie, to work out arrangements that met with general approval.

Over the next few months the couples began working together more easily with issues involving Millie. In turn, Millie's anxiety and depression slowly improved, and she reported that her father had told her everything really worked better for everyone now.

14. There Are Ambiguous Family Boundaries with Little Agreement as to Family Membership.

Boss and Greenberg (1984) have studied ambiguous loss for many years and identified the family stresses that can occur. The ambiguity in a stepfamily is not related to parents missing in action or being physically present but psychologically absent due to Alzheimer's disease, as in some of the families Boss and Greenberg studied. Instead it occurs because there often is little agreement between family members as to who is in the family (Pasley, 1987). In addition, constant changes in the composition of the household when children move back and forth between households adds an ambiguous element.

In many stepfamilies, children do not list stepparents as family members, and nonresidential parents omit their children from their list even though these children may spend time with that parent. Stepgrandparents also may not be included. Sometimes, children draw or list their two households as one family group, usually to the discomfort of the new couple, at the same time stepsiblings are excluded from the pictures. As a result, communication can suffer since individuals may be conceptualizing "family" references in different ways, and emotions can be strong in those left out, or in those who are expected to include as members persons they don't consider within the family boundaries.

Ambiguous boundaries also create discomfort by reducing predictability, thus lowering the sense of control that stepfamily members wish to have over their lives. Suddenly, they are confronted with incongruities of a very basic nature. It is important for therapists to be sensitive to the existence of this type of stress and not inadvertently add their own conceptualization of the family member-ship to what already may be a multifaceted concept.

15. Initially There Is No Family History.

When stepfamily members begin living together, they may, as yet, have no family history. Time is an essential ingredient in its development, and patience, understanding, and respectful communication help determine the content of that history. As this history unfolds, day-to-day activi-ties and special ways of doing things become familiar. Thus, predictability can bring a welcome relaxation within the family as members gain a sense of mastery in their lives.

Belonging to a group grows out of familiarity with the history and rituals of the group. Therapy can be extremely valuable in helping stepfamilies fill in their past histories for one another, develop new rituals for the new unit, and decide on former rituals that the family wishes to adopt or modify.

In one family who were about to have their first Christ-mas together, violent arguments arose over the plans for the day. Both adults had children, and they were all to be with Sheila and Harry for Christmas afternoon and evening. Sheila and her two children were used to opening their presents during the afternoon, while Harry and his three children had always made a game of present-opening later in the day. In Harry's previous household large presents for each child were found by following their special string that Harry had wound around table legs, under chairs, and through one room into the next. When Sheila said during a family therapy appointment, "I'm really into Christmas, but that seems like just too much," Harry's children began to cry. The therapist helped the family to take turns talking about their wishes for the day, and then helped them work out a plan which involved a somewhat restricted "cobweb" idea, plus the fun Sheila and her children had developed by taking turns choosing the next special present to be opened.

At this point the children visibly relaxed and accepted and enlarged on the new ritual. Sharing this part of their background had allowed them to continue talking together about their feelings and also allowed them to work out a plan of action that was acceptable to everyone. It takes time to develop stepfamily "history."

Helping stepfamily members share the likes, dislikes, and past rituals they have appreciated lays the groundwork for more understanding between the individuals. In this way, they can feel more comfortable together and not view the changes as a judgement that their former rituals were somehow "wrong." With this shared history, they can build on their past by developing satisfying ways of doing things in the new family situation.

16. The Emotional Climate Is Intense and Unexpected.

Many of the situations that arise in stepfamilies can also arise in other types of families. However, the emotional reactions are usually exaggerations of those felt in other types of families. This heightened emotional climate creates a different context within which the family is operating, and it has the following important therapeutic implications:

- Strong emotional responses need not be signals of individual or family pathology. They may be common reactions of individuals in stepfamilies still struggling with integration issues.
- Members may not be supportive of one another because they have little energy or empathy to put into understanding their own or other members' emotional responses.
- The household may be too volatile to be seen together because members may say hurtful things that cannot be "taken back." Seeing individuals or appropriate subgroups together may be a more productive approach.
- While other types of families may need the therapist to motivate change by consciously eliciting

stronger emotion during therapy sessions, stepfamilies may need the opposite interventions from
the therapist, namely a dampening down of the
emotional climate.

Frequently, stepfamily adults are upset and ashamed of
their responses in their new family. A stepfather of two
children confided to his therapist, "Sometimes, I become
so upset I find myself acting like a five-year-old. I may yell
at my wife or sit on the stairs and cry with frustration." In
another family, a 25-year-old stepdaughter felt ashamed
because she resented her new stepmother and felt jealous
of the attention her father was paying to his new wife's 16-
year-old daughter.

Therapists who have little experience with stepfamily
life sometimes feel overwhelmed with the strength of the
feelings expressed. They also may have an urge to label an
upset person in pathological terms. Try to withhold judgment. At the beginning, there is chaos and stress in most
stepfamilies. It is to be expected, and strong emotional
reactions to all the changes and confusion are also to be
expected. In fact, one of the positive things in working
with stepfamilies is the fact that with support, validation
of their feelings, and information on what is going on and
how to deal with it, many very emotional families settle
down surprisingly quickly.

First, stepfamily members need to feel the acceptance
and support of the therapist. When their self-esteem is
adequate and their responses are requiring less emotional energy, helping remarried parents and stepparents understand each other and understand their children
becomes important. Discussing the ways in which early
stepfamily life does little to satisfy the basic psychological needs discussed in Chapter 2 can help develop empathy. Reading and talking with others in stepfamily
situations also can be a useful adjunct to therapy. Clients can hear things from understanding peers that cannot
be said in a therapist's office, and clients' reactions to what

others are telling them can be discussed in the therapy session.

When Hal and Dee came for therapy, both were emotionally needy. They were not able to support one another; in fact, they were sometimes physically violent towards each other. The therapist did not see their children at the same time as the couple because the adults' relationship seemed too fragile and their emotions too strong to make it productive. In fact, they were seen individually three or four times for every time they were seen together.

These individual sessions allowed the therapist to support Hal and Dee in their overwhelming need for validation and support, and their times together furnished important glimpses of major stepfamily difficulties that could be addressed separately during individual sessions. Slowly they grew more confident and accepting of the situation and of themselves. Hal began to set limits with his former wife and Dee became less anxious and more supportive of Hal.

As these changes were made, and as their emotional outbursts lessened, they began to see their therapist together more frequently. They had become mutually supportive and had less need for individual sessions. They had individual issues from the past that were interfering with their adjustment to living in a remarriage family, but their new understanding of each other made it possible for them to listen to each other without escalating emotions. Very slowly, issues were resolved and the family settled down.

Such strong emotions are common until the initial chaos subsides, and knowing this helps the clients as well as the therapist. Indeed, one of the rewards of working with stepfamilies is the marked de-escalation of emotions that often occurs relatively quickly.

SUMMARY

This chapter outlines important differences between stepfamilies and first-marriage families and their consequent implications for therapy. Paying attention to these characteristics helps therapists carry in their thinking a family model different from that of a nuclear family and allows them to be more sensitive and understanding to what is taking place. This understanding, in turn, builds trust and makes the therapy sessions a safe place for stepfamily members to communicate with one another. As with most therapy, warmth and understanding is the foundation of effective therapy.

4

AREAS OF DIFFICULTY

The difficulties that occur in remarriage families can also occur in other types of families, although usually to a lesser degree. The basic source of the problems, however, is different. Initially, in stepfamilies the *external structural characteristics* discussed in Chapter 2 can produce a number of difficulties. In first-marriage families, the same types of problems occur usually because of *internal characteristics* of the individuals in the family. For example, a father with low self-esteem stemming from a background of neglect and rejection in his own family of origin might find it painful in a first-marriage family when his daughter runs into the arms of her mother, neglecting him. As a nonresidential father in a stepfamily, he would probably find his daughter's coolness towards him and her loyalty to her mother, who is now living elsewhere, extremely difficult to handle.

The following eight areas can cause difficulty in newly formed remarriage families regardless of the individual characteristics of family members:

1. Change and loss
2. Unrealistic beliefs
3. Insiders/outsiders
4. Life-cycle discrepancies
5. Loyalty conflicts
6. Boundary problems
7. Power issues
8. Closeness/distance

1. CHANGE AND LOSS

All changes bring loss, as the familiar is replaced by the unfamiliar. Remarriage is no exception, because it is a transition that brings with it much promise and also numerous losses, some acknowledged and expected and others not recognized or anticipated. In their pink cloud of anticipation, adults usually expect the children to be as enthusiastic as they are, and they do not recognize how many losses the children are experiencing. An only child may have become one of three, or the oldest may become a middle child. Children used to having rooms of their own may be asked to share their living space with stepsiblings; a request to share their toys may produce a negative response. To a child, a half-hour change in bedtime can be a dramatic shift, and the need to share a parent with a new partner and perhaps with stepsiblings can be a loss of parental time and attention that goes unnoticed and unacknowledged by adults. Helping the parent and stepparent develop some understanding and recognition of these and other losses for the children can do a great deal to help the family.

Kyle and Cynthia had been married for 10 months and, according to Kyle, "The children are driving us to distraction." Cynthia had one child, Ann, age 7, and Kyle had a daughter, Sandra, age 8, and a son, Tim, who was 6. (See Exhibit 4.1.) Ann lived with Kyle and Cynthia most of the time, and Kyle's children were with them three weekends each month and for a month during the summer. When the children were together there was constant fighting.

The following outline is a pattern of inquiry and interaction that the therapist followed to explore what was happening in the family:

1. Ascertain the concerns that bring Kyle and Cynthia in at this time.

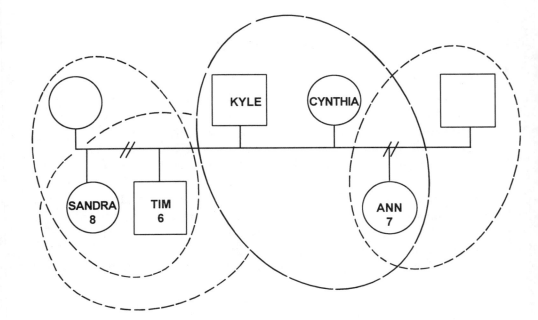

Exhibit 4.1. Kyle and Cynthia's Stepfamily.

2. Obtain necessary family history. (Drawing a genogram is an excellent way to gain important historical material.)

- How long have Kyle and Cynthia been together?
- How long have they been married?
- What are the sexes and ages of the children, and which adult is the biological parent of each of them?
- Do the children see their other parent? On what schedule?
- What are the children's living arrangements when they are with Kyle and Cynthia?
- What changes in household arrangements occur as children go back and forth between households?
- How do the children's two households relate to each other?

3. Inquire about important details regarding the children's fighting.

The therapist learned that the children fought constantly whenever the three of them were together. He also learned that when Kyle's children were with them, Ann needed to share her bedroom with Sandra, while Tim slept on a couch in the family room. All the children had an eight o'clock bedtime. This meant that Sandra's bedtime was a half hour earlier than it was at her mother's house. When they were all together, the adults planned a series of special family activities such as roller skating, going to the park, and swimming at a lake in the summer; but during the weekend when only Ann was there, few outings were planned. The activities consisted primarily of taking care of neglected household chores.

The therapist recognized that Cynthia and Kyle had little awareness of the many losses their children were experiencing and he suggested changes the couple could make that might shift the family in positive directions without needing to involve other family members in therapy. The therapist helped the couple become more sensitive to their children's losses as he helped them to understand the following points:

- That the children might be showing their anger at their losses by their behavior, rather than by talking about their feelings.

Losses for Ann:
- That Ann would suddenly lose contact with her mother and stepfather when Tim and Sandra were in the house because they received most of the attention from the adults and were treated as though they were visitors.
- That Ann also had to share her room with Sandra when the children were visiting, and this might be upsetting to her.
- That to Ann it probably appeared that her step-

siblings were loved more because the family did special things only when they were there.

Losses for Tim and Sandra:

- Tim and Sandra were missing special times they had been used to having earlier with their father at his apartment before his remarriage.
- Sandra might feel she had been "demoted" because she now was expected to go to bed at the same time as the two younger children, rather than staying up until her usual bedtime.
- Tim could feel that there was no place for him because he slept on the couch in the family room and had no special spot of his own.

As Cynthia and Kyle began to change how they interacted with their children, the children responded positively:

- Cynthia and Kyle arranged special one-on-one times with each child, reading a story, taking a walk, or playing a game. This helped build new relationships and maintain the parent—child relationships that had existed prior to the remarriage.
- The couple talked with all the children about their not having individual space, and planned together what private space Sandra and Tim could have that was *theirs* all the time, not just during their visiting times. (For many children it can simply be a drawer of their own for their clothes and toys.)
- In contrast to the weekend plans they had been making, when Tim and Sandra were with them, the family occasionally held "work weekends" for household chores, and at other times, when only Ann was there, she and Kyle and Cynthia planned a special family outing.
- When the adults discussed bedtime arrange-

ments with Sandra, her displeasure melted away as she recognized it was more fun to go to bed at the same time as Ann, rather than slipping into the room later on after Ann was asleep.

As a result of the changes, tension between the children dissipated and the couple no longer needed therapeutic help. However, they parted with the understanding that more assistance would be available to them should they wish to consult with their therapist again in the future.

Losses for adults in the new stepfamily can include many things: less time and space, loss of familiar surroundings, job changes, and separation from friends and family. The dream of a carefree first marriage may have disappeared; for a person who has not been married before, marrying someone with children can puncture the idealized bubble of "my family just being me and my husband and our children."

2. UNREALISTIC BELIEFS

These are three important myths that interfere with progress toward satisfactory stepfamily integration:

- Stepfamilies are the same as first-marriage families
- Stepfamily adjustment will take only a short time
- Loving and caring for one another will develop instantaneously

The greater the discrepancy between the couple's rosy expectations and the sobering reality, the more disappointed and upset they usually become. Unfortunately, many men and women enter remarriage with these and other unrealistic expectations and they quickly become disillusioned, guilty, and self-accusatory when the chaos in the new stepfamily does not calm down:

One stepmother, Candice, came to therapy because she was having great difficulty with her stepdaughter. Candice had been married for eight months to John, a man with two children, 11-year-old Marcia and Donald, 8. Candice was 38 and had never been married before—this was to be "her family." She had expected them all to be "one big happy family" within a few months following her marriage. She tried very hard to forge a relationship with Marcia and with Donald. According to Candice, her stepson responded warmly, but her stepdaughter grew increasingly angry. Candice was bewildered and wondered what she was doing wrong.

As Candice talked, she revealed her unrealistic beliefs about her stepfamily. Even though the children saw their mother every third weekend, Candice had an idealized picture of a nuclear family in her thoughts and expected the members of her new family unit to be immediately bound together by bonds of love and caring.

When the therapist gently attempted to point out differences between Candice's stepfamily and a first-marriage family, Candice became depressed. Then she grew angry and talked about stopping therapy. When the therapist acknowledged the sadness of letting go of her expectations for the family, Candice began to cry and then to talk more about her many disappointments in the family.

It is difficult to relinquish beliefs as important as those held by Candice. She very slowly accepted the differences between her family and a first-marriage family. She also accepted a more realistic view that stepfamily integration typically is a lengthy process but with increasing satisfaction and many rewards as new relationships become solid. Then her depression and anger subsided and she relaxed in her interactions with Marcia. Six months after her last therapy session, the therapist met Candice on the street. With great excitement Candice said, "I can hardly believe it, but the minute I relaxed and didn't push Marcia she stopped being so rebellious, and now we have fun together. It's been really great!"

In situations in which the adults in stepfamilies are disappointed with each other, asking them about their expectations of one another can be very revealing and helpful. Even more helpful is the "homework" task of writing down separately the following information to share with one another at the next therapy appointment:

1. Please list your expectations of your partner and of your family.
2. Please write after each expectation whether you consider it to be realistic or unrealistic.

As they compare their lists, couples are often able to laugh at some of their beliefs, discarding them in favor of expectations that are more realistic for their particular family unit.

3. INSIDERS/OUTSIDERS

In Chapter 2, we talked about the way in which stepfamily structure initially does not meet the very basic human need that we all have, to feel that we belong to a group at work, at home, or in social situations. For instance, when a single man or woman marries someone who has children, he or she is joining an already existing group of people. The couple may be comfortable together, but when the family is present, the remarried parent and child or children have a history together and are "insiders" who can read each other's moods, words, and actions. The stepparent is a stranger in the group.

In some remarriage families both adults may have children and when the stepfamily is together there are two separate subgroups attempting to share the same space.

When one subgroup moves into the home of the other group, the new group encroaches on the space of the original subgroup. As one new husband and father of a 10-year-old said, "My stepdaughters are nice little girls, but they invade my space. My son and I feel inundated." On the other hand, the girls and their mother also feel like intruders. Clearly, if at all possible, a new stepfamily needs to try to reduce turf battles and feelings of being outsiders by starting out in a new home. While a few families can overcome this obstacle to integration, the usual scenario is one in which the family finally moves into its own home after the trial of a number of chaotic and unhappy months.

The need to belong is very basic:

In the case of the Fielding family, Clarice Fielding was the one who called for an appointment with the therapist. She had moved into her husband's home nine months earlier when she and Derek were married. Derek had been a widower for two years and he and his three children had continued to live in their large home in a rural area. As Clarice spoke of her situation, she became so upset she could hardly speak. Through her tears, she painted the following verbal picture:

Clarice: When my son Ted and I moved in there was no place for us. Nobody had thought to clear some drawers for us, and of course there was no place for any of our furniture. I sold most of it but I wanted to keep a few special things. We stored them in the basement of Derek's house. Derek's daughter had a room of her own, and now his twin boys have to share their room with Ted. They hated that. I even found some of Derek's former wife's clothes in the drawers in *our* bedroom. Alicia saw me take them out and she began to cry at seeing her mother's things. It was awful.

I still don't feel as though Ted and I have any place there and my husband doesn't understand it. He is very attached to the house and he doesn't want to move his children. As he says, it's the house they grew up in. He gets angry at me for not appreciating the comfortable space we have. Our relationship is getting worse all the time.

Therapist: So you and Ted keep feeling as though you don't really belong there.

Clarice: Yes, yes, that's right, and if I move anything Derek's children are upset.

The therapist, with Clarice's permission, called Derek to speak with him directly:

Therapist: I understand you and your wife are having difficulty understanding each other's feelings about the home you're living in.

Derek: That's right. It's a beautiful place but Clarice doesn't seem to like it.

Therapist: It would be helpful if I could hear the way you feel about it. Would you be willing to come in and talk with me so I could get a clearer picture?

The therapist met with Derek alone for a session during which Derek talked about his home and his children:

Derek: I love the house. My former wife and I built it after living in a tiny apartment for six years. We both worked hard to make it possible. That was ten years ago. My daughter was only two when we moved there and the twins have never lived anywhere else. Naturally they were very upset when their mother died and the house means a lot to all of us.

Therapist: It must be difficult having Clarice and Ted not feel the same way about it.

Derek: Yes. It's much nicer than anything they've ever had before.

The therapist was able to see Derek and Clarice together and help them discuss each other's feelings—Derek's fear of loss and Clarice's feeling of alienation. Through new understanding, the couple grew closer to each other, and with this bonding they were able to work together on a solution.

After talking about redecorating or remodeling, they decided to see what was available in the same area in which they were living. When they became committed to moving, they included the children in their planning and pointed out that they were looking for a house with more bedrooms. This was a positive move as far as the boys were concerned. When they finally purchased a new home, they asked the children to help decide how they wished to decorate their rooms. There was sadness in the move, but the adults had not proceeded precipitously and the gradual transition had been helpful for Derek and his children. The anticipation of a change had made the waiting more acceptable to Clarice and Ted.

Even when stepfamilies start out in a place of their own, there are still subgroups with preexisting alliances and they are the "insiders." Helping the newcomers work their way into the family system is an important aspect of early stepfamily life. Parent–child coalitions usually do remain in stepfamilies even when the family gains an identity and sense of belonging together. However, a couple alliance is most necessary and integration cannot occur in the presence of separate insider and outsider groups.

It is through positive shared memories that relationships form and already existing relationships are maintained. After a remarriage, children need to have some special time alone with their parent to maintain the close bond they share. In addition, a stepparent and the stepchildren also need special exclusive times together to build their new relationships. Family times and memories are important, but they are not a substitute for the bonding that takes place on a one-to-one basis. A major way in which to develop group cohesiveness is to develop productive and enjoyable family rituals, ways of doing things that involve everyone in the household. Rituals reinforce family roles and rules and bind individuals together by providing shared expectations and memories. A family identity evolves and the members are clear about their participation. Family members gain the sense that they belong.

There are many examples of both simple and complex stepfamily rituals that can become models to stimulate the thinking of other families in introducing important rituals for their families. In one stepfamily in which both adults had children, when the children received their weekly allowances, they were given them by their stepparent rather than by their parent. In another instance, each of the five children chose the menu for one of the weekday evening meals. In still another family, birthdays were celebrated with a special theme party that included games as well as favors, decorations, and a fancy birthday cake. As McGoldrick has said, "It is extremely important to reinforce a family's use of rituals so as to reinforce their sense of identity" (Carter & McGoldrick, 1988, p. 83).

4. LIFE-CYCLE DISCREPANCIES

In first marriages, there are two adults who have similar marriage and family experiences. Both are married at the same time, and for the same length of time. They become parents at the same moment, and their family is at least as old as the oldest child. As a rule, the couple will be fairly close in age, and perhaps starting their working lives about the same time. In remarriages, however, the marriage and family history of the adults may be very different, and the children are not joining the family as newborns.

Linda and Bob are a clear example of the discrepancies that can exist. After 16 years of marriage, Bob was divorced. His son Joe was 14 at the time. Three years

later, Bob and Linda were married. Linda was 30, had
never been married before, and was just beginning a
new job as a legal secretary that she was enjoying very
much. Bob was 18 years older than Linda and his
career as a very successful attorney had allowed him
to move into a solo practice with the luxury of working only four days a week. Bob owned a 26-foot
sailboat on which he spent most of his free time. Bob
continually urged Linda to sail with him, even on the
few weekends when he had his son Joe with him to
help with the handling of the boat. Linda didn't often
accept these invitations. She didn't enjoy sailing, and
felt it conflicted with her job, which was very important to her. She also did not enjoy being with her
stepson Joe, with whom she had not formed a good
relationship. After three years of marriage, the stress
between Linda and Bob had increased to the point
where Linda sought therapeutic help.

During her first appointment Linda's frustration
and upset came tumbling forth through her tears:

> She did not like sailing very much, but she was
> willing to go once or twice a month with Bob for a
> day or two. Her work at the law firm was going very
> well. She continued to enjoy her job and was given
> new responsibilities, which she appreciated. How-
> ever, she did not feel she could take Fridays off to
> sail with Bob, and she was becoming more and
> more upset with his pressure on her to do so; at the
> same time she felt guilty that she did not want to
> accompany Bob on his outings. Linda was also
> feeling guilty because her relationship with Joe, her
> stepson, was not close.
>
> The therapist acknowledged Linda's pain and
> commented that there are greater discrepancies in
> remarriages simply because all parties are at very
> different places in their life cycles. Linda was at the
> beginning of her career, while her husband was at a
> place where he no longer wished to work as hard as
> was necessary at the beginning of his career.

Then the therapist turned to the topic of Joe:

Therapist: Does Joe spend considerable time
with his friends?

Linda: Yes, he and his friends do things together
most weekends, so we don't see him very often. I
don't think he likes me much. He's polite, but he
doesn't talk a lot when he's with us.

Therapist: When you were Joe's age, what kind
of activities did you have?

Linda: I was a cheerleader for our school football
team. We had a lot of fun. We'd practice a lot
and five of us did a lot of other things together. It
was great!

Therapist: Did you talk to your parents a lot
then?

Linda: No, not really. I was so busy at school,
and I had a lot of homework to do. Then on the
weekends we had the games.

The therapist was able to help Linda see the simi-
larities between her interests during her teen years
and Joe's present interests. Linda began to understand
that Joe was at a developmental place in his life in
which his relationships with peers were very important. These maturational needs did not match with
Linda's wish to develop a new family unit. When
Linda could understand that Joe's behavior did not
necessarily reflect on her, she relaxed and began to
enjoy the little time they did have together.

With Linda's permission, the therapist contacted
Bob and suggested it might be helpful if he came for an
appointment so that the therapist would know what
his concerns were. Bob did come in and he talked
about his wish to share his leisure time with Linda,
and his deep concern about the tension in their relationship. During this session the therapist helped Bob
understand the need for negotiation because of the
differences that existed between Bob and his wife due

to the discrepancies in their life cycles. Following these individual appointments it took months of couple appointments for Linda and Bob to work out ways to deal creatively with their differences.

One other potential difference—whether or not to have a child together—did not arise for this couple, at least at this time. Frequently, when one of the couple has children and the other does not, there is a clash because the one who has no children wishes to have a child and the other does not. In therapy, working out a solution to these discrepant needs can be a lengthy process. Sometimes, other basic issues are involved. At other times, the individual who wants the child agrees not to expect help in caring for the child, and once in awhile couples even separate over this issue despite the fact that there is considerable love between them.

5. LOYALTY CONFLICTS

In functional first-marriage families when a child is born, the couple has already developed a strong bond. Bonding with the infant often takes place quickly. When members of a stepfamily come together, routinely there are preexisting parent–child alliances and a newer couple relationship that needs to be developed and nourished. In addition, there are children, not only connected to a parent in that household, but also with bonds to another parent living elsewhere (or in their memory if the parent has died). There is also the need for the children and their parent's new partner to develop their relationships. No wonder that many remarriage families have to deal with uncomfortable loyalty conflicts.

Often, individuals understand their situation by seeing the schematic diagrams that appear on page 38 concerning relationships in a new and integrated stepfamily. One therapist talking to a new couple about their emotional needs also drew a diagram similar to Exhibit 2.2 that showed their particular bonding pattern. In this new stepfamily was the mother and her two children, while the stepfather with no children was connected only to his wife. He felt validated and understood when the therapist commented on his position, and his wife could empathize with his feelings of being left out as she looked at all the connections she had in the family. Diagrams can be effective communicators.

These diagrams can also lead to discussion of competing loyalties. For example, remarried parents often feel caught between love for their children and feelings for their new spouse, and many adults consider that forming a strong couple relationship is a betrayal of their relationship with their children. Children worry about liking their stepparent because they think that caring about a new adult means that they are being disloyal to their biological parent. Children often feel that the amount of love a person has to give is limited rather than being infinite in quantity. Even adults can feel this way. One remarried father said, "I considered I had one bucket full of love, and if I gave some of it to my stepchildren this would leave less for my own children." Fortunately, he learned the truth from an observation made by a remarried mother when she remarked, "The children taught us there's enough love to go around."

As we said in Chapter 2, the desire to be cared about and loved is a basic need in human beings. Unfortunately, many parents fear they will lose closeness with their children if the children feel positively about their stepparents, and many remarried parents fear the loss of closeness with their children if they build strong relationships with their new partners or with their stepchildren. Unfortunately, adults' responses to these fears can exacerbate children's loyalty conflicts that may already be of concern to the children.

The following scenarios illustrate three common types of loyalty issues. The first is the case of Dee, which illustrates the dilemma for a remarried mother who is also a stepmother.

Hal and Dee had been married for two years. This was a second marriage for each of them, and Hal's fear of not seeing his two girls had resulted in an inability to set limits in his contact with his former wife, Linda. She would call him frequently at work and in the evenings when he was home, to discuss inconsequential details about the girls. Also, nearly every month she would ask Hal for money beyond his child support payments, and Hal would agree to her requests despite the hardship this created for himself and Dee. Dee felt insecure in her relationship with Hal and kept accusing him of still loving Linda.

During six months of therapy, both worked hard to improve their relationship. They were now supporting one another; Hal had set limits with Linda, and Dee was supportive rather than combative with her husband.

At this point, Dee became concerned about her role as a stepmother to her stepchildren, who were with Hal and Dee frequently. Hal assured Dee that he felt his daughters appreciated her and that she was doing a good job in her role as a stepmother. Dee, however, could not accept Hal's evaluation and the therapist suggested that Dee have an appointment alone to talk about the dilemma.

During this separate session, in response to the therapist's questions, Dee identified a number of troublesome emotions:

1. Guilt that she doesn't feel the same about her younger stepdaughter as she does about her biological son
2. Need to make sure that her son knows that no other child will threaten her relationship with him

At this point Dee commented, "Not knowing what my role with my stepdaughter is gets worse the more I like her." This comment alerted the therapist to a possible loyalty conflict different from the one Dee was consciously talking about.

> *Therapist:* It sounds as though you also are worried that you might grow to love your step-daughter more than you love your son. After all, your son is on his own now and you see your stepdaughter a lot more.
>
> *Dee (through tears):* That does scare me. I don't want that to happen.

Dee and Hal had both talked to the therapist previously about their perception that Dee's older sister had been, and was still, the favorite of her parents, while Dee was not accepted by them. Thus the therapist already had the necessary information to continue:

> *Therapist:* I remember you told me that your parents loved your sister more than they loved you.
>
> *Dee:* Yes, that's right.
>
> *Therapist:* So you've not had the experience of seeing parents who love two children.
>
> *Dee:* No, I haven't.
>
> *Therapist:* Perhaps that's why you can't imagine that you could continue to love your son if you also loved your stepdaughter.
>
> *Dee (after some thought):* Maybe that's true.

Another individual session a week later reinforced this explanation and Dee slowly relaxed when she discovered that she did not resemble her parents in this way. In this example, a common stepparent fear was exacerbated by her childhood experience in her family of origin.

The second example concerned Jim, the father of an older girl and two younger boys. Jim was remarried to

Lisa, a woman who was not married before. Jim and
Lisa had been married for six years, and during that
time Lisa felt that Jim's allegiance to his children
remained as the primary relationship and that a true
allegiance to her had not developed. Jim felt the need
to protect his children from their mother's negligence,
and he also feared that they would be angry at him if
he did not attempt to meet all their demands. As a
result, Lisa's needs were not considered. She became
depressed and had withdrawn from Jim.

After almost a year of therapy in which this area of
concern was explored in detail, Jim's response to an
all-too-common interaction between his daughter and
Lisa helped move the family into a new level of
functioning. Jim and Lisa had picked up Jim's daughter, Margo, after her music lesson. She was coming to
their home for the weekend and they were going to
have something to eat on their way home. As the three
of them drove away from her music teacher's home,
Margo made a cutting remark to Lisa. At this point,
Jim stopped the car and said to his daughter, "It hurts
me when you speak to my wife that way. I love you
both and it makes me feel sad when you speak to Lisa
like that, and you do it quite often." Margo began to
cry and so did Lisa. Then Lisa and Margo began to talk
together about their feelings—primarily Lisa's hurt
and Margo's fear that her growing affection for Lisa
would hurt her mother.

Usually this type of conversation cannot take place
until the children realize that their remarried parent
has formed an alliance with his or her new spouse; at
the same time, the remarried parent continues to care,
as before, about the needs of his or her children. Jim
had not supported Lisa in front of Margo before, and
his statement that he loved both of them was an
important element in giving both Margo and Lisa the
message that as far as his love was concerned it was not
an either/or situation, but one that included both of
them. Not only were Lisa and Margo no longer in

competition for Jim's affection, but also Jim was no longer caught in a loyalty bind between them.

The final example is one involving Kevin, an upset 10-year-old who said to his therapist, "I love my Mom and my Dad, I want to keep them both happy, and I can't. There's nothing I can do. I've got a stepfather and my Mom wants me to like him. If I do I'm afraid it will hurt my Dad, and I don't want to hurt my Dad."

In this example, Kevin agreed to allow his therapist to talk with his dad and also with his mom and stepfather about his feelings. After the therapist had two separate sessions with them, the three adults agreed to meet together with Kevin in an attempt to resolve their difficulties because of their love for him. The therapist scheduled the appointment so that Kevin would be coming during a time he was with his dad. In this way, there was a balance between the four coming to the session: Kevin and his father, and his mom and stepfather. During this meeting, the adults assured Kevin they all cared about him. His parents spoke about their love for him and said they knew he loved them. His father also told Kevin that he thought that Kevin and his stepfather could have good times together and get to really care about each other, maybe even love each other. He let Kevin know this was acceptable as far as he was concerned because he knew Kevin would continue to love him.

When parents speak and behave in ways that let children know that it is all right with them for the children to care about, enjoy, and learn from the adults in their other household, it removes, or at least reduces, their child's loyalty conflicts.

6. BOUNDARY PROBLEMS

As a rule, first-marriage families have distinct family boundaries around their household, and also boundaries between adults and children within the household. Individuals within the household agree as to who is in the family. In contrast, as pointed out in Chapter 3, there are many ambiguous boundaries in remarriage families and the individuals involved do not always agree about just who is in the family. While there needs to be a firm boundary around the household, there also needs to be gates in the wall for the children to pass through as they go back and forth between their two parental homes. Boss and Greenberg (1984) believe that ambiguous family boundaries bring stress to families. With more ambiguous stepfamily boundaries, it is not surprising that many stepfamilies have boundary difficulties. Often, a major therapeutic task is to help strengthen important stepfamily boundaries, particularly the boundary around the couple and the boundaries between the children's two households.

The Fitzgerald family illustrates a common boundary problem in stepfamilies involving the new couple and the children.

Meg and John had been married for 10 months and the couple sought help because of frequent arguments and an erosion of their originally warm and intimate relationship. The therapist saw the couple alone, although Meg had wanted to include her two daughters. John had not been married previously and was finding it difficult to be the only male in an otherwise all female household. Even the cat was a female!

As the therapist explored the situation with the couple, he saw the lack of a clear boundary around the couple. The two girls, Sheila, age 8, and Tammie, age 10, had been used to having the run of the house during the three years they had lived primarily with their mother in a single-parent household. After Meg's remarriage, the girls continued to come into Meg and John's bedroom unannounced, and they often turned on the TV in the adults' bedroom and flopped onto the bed to watch it there rather than in the living room. Meg had asked Sheila and Tammie to knock when the door was closed, but the girls often "forgot." This did not particularly bother Meg, but John was becoming more angry and resentful about the adults' lack of privacy. He felt left out of the conversations between his wife and her daughters, and also was missing private and intimate times with his new wife.

The therapist made it clear that he could identify with the feelings of each adult, and then he was able to help the couple accept the differences in each other's feelings. With mutual understanding, the couple reached compromises and worked out ways in which they could provide a space and time for the couple that would be separate from Tammie and Sheila. They decided that until 8:30 p.m. their bedroom could be a gathering spot for them all to talk together, but not to watch TV unless the adults allowed it. After that time, even on weekends, the door would be closed and Meg and John would have time to themselves, just the two of them. They put a sign on the door at 8:30 which said, "Do not knock unless you're bleeding," as a humorous reminder for the girls.

Tammie and Sheila each had her own bedroom, and at times they also wanted their privacy. The couple pointed out that adults had similar needs and that was what was prompting the changes. At first, the girls complained bitterly, but once it was a couple decision that their mother supported they slowly grew used to the changes. A much needed boundary had been drawn between the adults and the children, reducing the boundary ambiguity in the household. John knew what he could count on and felt that Meg respected their time alone. With this clarification, they began to once again find time to be together in a warm and loving manner.

A second important boundary that can create severe difficulties for stepfamily members is a lack of separation between the children's two households. At times, this is due to the fact that remarried parents fear that creating an adequate boundary will anger the former spouse, who will then retaliate by not allowing the children to visit their other household. At other times, a psychological separation has not been completed and the two households are held together by anger, or by the remarried parent's inability to let go of the former relationship. Unfortunately, in either situation, difficulties are created for the children and for the new partner. When anger remains, the children often are caught between their parents, and when remarried parents are not able to say goodbye to a former partner, these adults are not able to commit fully to a new spouse.

Although it is desirable for the two adults in households to form a "parenting coalition" (Visher & Visher, 1989) to work cooperatively on raising the children, if this connection occurs without adequate separateness between the two households it does not work smoothly. Typically, the remarried spouse who is still psychologically attached to a former spouse will unconsciously promote connections between the children's two households, usually around issues or conversations having little bearing on the joint task of raising the children. This was the situation for Bart and Linda.

> During a first therapy session, Bart related how much the behavior of his ex-wife was causing difficulty in his present marriage. His former wife, Betty, would frequently call him at work or during the evening shortly before Bart and Linda were getting into bed. Linda was particularly upset with the calls because it disturbed the couple's time alone together. She was also disturbed because Bart would often talk with Betty about situations having nothing to do with his children. He would mention his complaints about conditions where he worked and make suggestions for Betty on ways she could work out a misunderstanding with a good friend of hers. On the other hand, Linda worked well with her former husband, but with little unnecessary contact or conversation.

The therapist complimented the couple on their ability to provide a nonhostile environment for all of their children and asked them about ways in which they could reduce the tension between the two of them. Both agreed that the contact between Bart and Betty was causing difficulty. Betty had also remarried, and they began to wonder about the interaction between her new husband and his reaction to Bart and Betty's phone relationship. The therapist inquired about the couple's families of origin and Bart spoke of the divorce of his parents and the continuing distress their hostility towards one another caused for him. He wished to protect his children from hostility such as he himself had experienced. Linda began to see her husband's behavior as coming from his concern for his children rather than from a lack of caring for her, and Bart began to realize he had "gone overboard" in his fear of angering Betty.

Slowly Bart discontinued discussions with Betty about areas which had little or no relevance to raising the children. He gradually reduced the number of times he talked with Betty by letting her know he could not talk with her when he was at work and setting restricted times for her to call when he was available at home. Bart also began to include Linda in most of the calls, and soon Betty's husband also participated. The two households continued to work together satisfactorily in their dealings with the children. In fact, their "parenting coalition" became even more effective when all four adults were more involved in discussions about the children. With clear boundaries around each household, all the adults were emotionally free to deal with the necessary parenting issues.

7. POWER ISSUES

In Chapter 2, we talked about the basic need for human beings to be in situations in which they have some personal control. We also indicated ways in which stepfamily structure did not meet that need. In fact, three of the major problems that bring stepfamilies into therapy are related to issues of control. They are: (1) dealing with former spouses, (2) discipline issues involving stepchildren, and (3) unacceptable behavior of the children (Pasley, Rhoden, Visher, & Visher, 1996). We have given a number of vignettes concerned with children's behavior. A discussion of the other two areas follows.

Dealing with Former Spouses

In stepfamilies the children have a parent elsewhere. If the parent has died, memories can exert a great deal of influence on the stepfamily household. If he or she is alive, various interactions reduce the autonomy of both households. With a joint physical custody arrangement there may be a more balanced power structure between the two households, while in situations where one parent is the residential parent and the other is a nonresidential or noncustodial parent, the residential households usually are the ones with the greater power.

The helplessness of nonresidential parents and their new spouses causes many of them to behave in uncharacteristic and unproductive ways. One such remarried father, for example, would not release his grip on the door handle of his former wife's car when she came to take his children away from his home on a weekend when it was his time to have them. Even though the car was moving and about to accelerate, he kept protesting and attempting to open the car door. Fortunately, no one was hurt; however, this man was reacting in an uncharacteristic and ineffective manner to the feelings of helplessness he was experiencing.

While nuclear families do not need to consider another household while making family decisions, remarriage families often need to work out plans with the children's other household. Arranging for summer vacations, for example, may take coordination between two households, and bringing a child for therapy may require the permission of the parent in the "other" household. Unfortunately, many adults react to this loss of autonomy by relinquishing more power than is necessary. In such cases the therapeutic task often becomes one of helping the adults to utilize productively the control they do have. Will and Carla were such a couple.

Will and Carla had been married for three years. Will had two children, Laura, nine, and Charlie, 11, who were with their mother, Judy, most of the time; their father and stepmother saw them on most weekends and for two weeks in the summer. Every year a major struggle occurred between the two households around the scheduling of the summer vacation. During the previous three summers, because of the arguments, Will and Carla had been unable to plan far enough in advance to have a vacation without several work-related appointments intruding during their vacation time.

It seemed to Will and Carla that whatever plans they made were sabotaged by the children's mother, and each year, they became more angry. When the couple sought outside help, the social worker suggested the possibility of the adults in both households coming together to work out the problem. Will and Carla did not wish to do this, but with therapeutic assistance they were able to take more control in the following way. They studied their summer commitments and arrived at three convenient times to have their vacation. Because Judy worked out of her home, and did her own scheduling, Carla and Will felt that Judy would have no difficulty deciding on her summer schedule. They believed that Judy appreciated two weeks for herself without the children; for this reason Will felt that Judy would be able to choose a time for the children to be away from her that would be of benefit to her as well. Will felt very nervous, because

he feared the possible loss of time with his children if
Judy became angry at him for taking the initiative to
change the way they had unsuccessfully arranged
summer plans. However, he realized that he needed
to take this risk because his fear of loss was reducing
his ability to take appropriate control in situations
involving his children. Since telephone conversations were generally not productive, he wrote the
following letter:

April 23

Dear Judy,

As we all know, we have had considerable difficulty these past few years working out suitable
times for our vacations with Laura and Charlie. It
may be helpful to plan this time further in advance
than before, so we have already scheduled our
summer commitments at work. As a result, we
know what times are available for us to be away
from our offices during the children's school vacation. These times are: June 21–July 5; July 16–July
31; or August 6–August 21.

We enjoy having the children go with us, and we
hope one of these dates will work well for you. If we
do not hear that any of these periods are suitable, it
will be disappointing for us to go without the
children, but that is what we would need to do this
year. If one of these dates is agreeable, please let us
know by May 25th because that is the latest date we
can arrange time to be away from work.

Regards,

Will

Judy did respond in time, as Will and Carla had
hoped she might, and the vacation plans were worked
out without the usual bickering and tension between
the two households. Carla and Will felt less helpless

and this allowed them to negotiate more effectively with Judy in the future.

Stepfamily Discipline

Discipline issues surface as one of the most troublesome stepfamily areas. Basically, this occurs because of gender stereotyping and little recognition of the stepparent's lack of power in connection with stepchildren prior to the development of a positive relationship between them.

In first-marriage families, parents have power in their role as parents that has derived naturally from their relationship. In stepfamilies, stepparents enter with no such authority and only through their efforts can they "earn" this type of power in the household. Although stepfamily couples have been found to have more egalitarian relationships than first-marriage couples (Kimball, 1988), even in these households many women still expect themselves, and may be expected by their husbands, to take a limit-setting role with their stepchildren. Until a relationship has developed this usually leads to frustration and tension within the household. Until children care about pleasing their stepparent, the adult has little to no authority as far as the children are concerned. It is the parent of the children who needs to remain in charge or learn to take charge of his or her children. This point is illustrated by the following case example:

Jeannie called for an appointment because she was depressed and angry, and also concerned about the schism developing between herself and her husband Tom. During her first appointment the therapist recorded the following information:

Jeannie and Tom had been married for ten months. Jeannie had not been married previously, and Tom had two children, Laura, 11, and Nickie, eight, from a previous marriage. The children's mother had been hospitalized for depression several times and the children had lived with Tom since shortly after his divorce. Tom disliked disciplining his children and when he remarried he made it clear that he expected Jeannie to take this responsibility. Jeannie loved children and had looked forward to becoming a "mother" to Tom's children. Not surprisingly, the family was not doing well.

Laura and Nickie were rude to Jeannie and refused to do what she said. When Jeannie complained to her husband, he talked with his children and they painted such a negative picture of their interactions with their stepmother that Tom felt it necessary to counsel his wife on the raising of children. He also brought two parenting books from the library for Jeannie to read. Instead of this improving the situation, the relationship between Jeannie and her stepchildren and also between Jeannie and her husband grew worse, and Jeannie had nowhere to turn for support because Tom was withdrawing from her and siding with his children.

The therapist spent several hours working with Jeannie alone. Her self-confidence was shaken and she needed to realize that her own expectations of suddenly taking on a parenting role with "half-grown children" were unrealistic. The therapist also suggested several books that helped Jeannie understand the need for stepparents—even when they had children of their own—to come into a stepfamily situation very gradually, and to not take a disciplinary role with their stepchildren.

After several appointments, the therapist talked about seeing the couple together, and with Jeannie's permission she called Tom and asked if he would come to the next appointment with his wife. Tom was willing to come, and the therapist very slowly directed the conversation toward the subject of parenting of the children. Tom had grown up in a family in which his mother had run the household and his

father had been a workaholic who related very super-
ficially to his children. Tom had no model of a father
who was active with his children, and he resisted
suggestions from the therapist about this topic. Tom
was, however, willing to read the stepfamily book that
Jeannie had found so helpful to her.

During the couple's next appointment Tom talked
of having some fun taking Laura and Nickie to the zoo
while Jeannie was busy elsewhere. With some enthu-
siasm, he said, "That book says that in our kind of
family I should be doing the disciplining of my children." (For some people, words in books have more
authenticity than words spoken by a therapist!) The
therapist nodded in agreement and together they
worked out what this might mean in their household.

In this family, Tom's shift toward taking control of his
children improved the situation with them and brought
the couple together. However, the children still were upset
and the therapist saw them with Tom and Jeannie for
several appointments. The children were beginning to like
Jeannie and were feeling disloyal to their mother. They
needed support from their father and stepmother to care
about all three adults in their lives, and they needed more
contact with their mother, who was living only a few miles
away from their home. Increasing this contact reduced the
tension still further in the household.

Of course there will be times when a stepparent is the
only adult who is with the children. What seems to work
is for the parent to delegate authority to the stepparent by
having the family meet together and saying to the children
something similar to: "We all know what the house rules
are, and when I'm not here and Marcie (stepmother) is here,
she is in charge. I expect you to do what she says."

At times when the stepparent has handled a situation in
the absence of the parent and the parent is not pleased with
the way his or her partner has dealt with the situation, the
parent needs to support the stepparent in front of the

children. Then later, the couple can get together privately and talk about different ways of reacting in similar situations in the future. As stepparent and stepchild form a respectful relationship, the stepparent can slowly begin to take on an independent disciplinary role.

8. CLOSENESS/DISTANCE

There is a self-consciousness about relationships in stepfamilies, and a tendency to feel guilty. If you do not love your stepchild you feel guilty; if you do love your stepchild you feel guilty—perhaps it means that you have taken love away from your biological child; and stepsiblings fight with each other to keep themselves from being emotionally drawn together.

Stepsiblings and stepparents may not have known each other for more than a few months while the parent and his or her children have been together since each child's birth. In first-marriage families, parent–child relationships are routinely taken for granted, while in a remarriage family they usually are observed, analyzed, and often critically reviewed by those within the family unit, and also by neighbors and friends. Within the household, the parent may pressure a new spouse to try to love his or her children, and children are expected to care about or love their stepparent. In fact, many adults push children to refer to their stepparent by a relationship term such as "Mom" or "Dad." Some variation of this, "Daddy Bill," for example, may work out for young children, but for older children it can feel like a demand to abandon the parent in their other household or in their memory. One 34-year-old man, for example, talked about his childhood relationship with his stepmother saying, "We really got along very well for several years. Then she asked me to call her 'Mother' and it was very tense and uncomfortable between us from that day on."

In contrast, some children ask a stepparent if they may use the term "Mom" or "Dad," or something similar. If the

adult denies this request, stepchildren report feeling rejected and upset. It is not a simple matter and it can be an
important topic of discussion in therapy. A noncustodial
parent may be offended by having another adult called
"Dad" by his child, and the child may not wish to reject a
biological parent by calling a stepparent by a relational
term. Helping the family to follow the children's lead
appears to be an important consideration in this matter. In
fact, therapists need to be careful to use appropriate language when working with this type of family. A sensitive
therapist during an initial meeting with a family in which
the wife had two children and the husband had three began
to address the concerns of family members. "What do you
call your stepparent?" he asked the children in a matter-of-
fact manner, and after their answers (all used first names
for their stepparent) he was careful to refer to the adults in
an approved and customary way for this family.

Later in the same session, a 16-year-old girl spoke of
feeling close and wanting to hug her 10-year-old stepbrother, but not being sure whether it would be OK. The
therapist asked the 10-year-old how he would feel if his
stepsister were to hug him, at which point the boy fell
backwards off his chair! Discomfort in a new relationship
and the normalcy of this reaction may be an important
theme in therapeutic interchanges.

More problematic are the emotions of teenagers of the
opposite sex who have not grown up together and who
suddenly find themselves living in a stepfamily household, one which is typically more sexually charged than an
original family household with children of a comparable
age. There is a new couple who may still be in the
"honeymoon stage," along with teenagers just getting to
know one another. Frequently, adults do not realize the
importance of helping their children by making new
rules—the establishment of a dress code, for example—or
by providing the children with as much privacy as possible. While children need the model of a couple that has
a loving and affectionate relationship, it is not helpful if the
couple displays passion outside the bedroom. Sexual

attractions certainly do occur in stepfamilies more frequently than in many other types of families because of
the emotional environment and because of the lack of
familiarity between steprelatives. Acknowledging this
possibility in therapy and differentiating between feelings and behavior may be important. Sexual feelings, if
acted upon, can be destructive to the household. Techni-
cally, such relationships between steprelatives are not
incestual, but as Margaret Mead commented, "There is
household incest," when the types of familial expectations
are disregarded.

Frank discussions with teenagers, when appropriate,
can reduce the pull of forbidden and secret emotions.
When stepteens do become emotionally attached, and the
relationship doesn't work out, because usual teenage problems arise, both adults are involved with *both* adolescents,
and there is no one for the teenagers to talk with about
feelings or the impasse in which they find themselves.
This type of situation does occur and therapeutic help can
be valuable, not only to provide young people with understanding, but also to help the family work out more
suitable living arrangements and behavioral guidelines.
For example, in one family a 20-year-old young man
became involved with his 17-year-old stepsister. Since he
was working outside the home, the adults helped him to
move into a small apartment of his own. He and his
stepsister continued to see each other, but not within a
household with three younger children. In another
stepfamily, the family room was converted into a bedroom
so that a 16-year-old girl and her 17-year-old stepbrother
did not have to share the same bathroom.

In other stepfamilies, over time truly loving relationships can and do form between adults and children.
Allowing bonds to form at their own pace increases the
likelihood that more permanent ties will result, while
pressure to pretend to care actually retards the growth
of caring relationships. Over time, bonds between step-

siblings can become important in the adult lives of children who have grown up together, and children often feel warmly towards stepparents only after they become young adults and are living on their own. At other times, adults look back and feel the way one young woman reported, "I was fortunate growing up in a stepfamily because I was part of two households and I had four adults to love me."

ADULT–CHILD RELATIONSHIPS

Relationships between mothers, fathers, and children in nuclear families have become the positive standard by which other family relationships are judged. This is in spite of the fact that these relationships range from very positive to very negative, just like those in other types of families.

Unfortunately, the myth of nuclear family perfection leads the adults in many stepfamilies to underestimate the warmth and importance of their step relationships. These step relationships are usually seen by stepfamily members as more distant than the mythical standard, and by society as "uncaring" as compared to relationships in "normal" families.

When step relationships become close, they are considered by many to have changed their status. The "step" designation is considered then to be incorrect, and a common expression is "she's become my daughter (or son)." Similarly, an unauthorized editorial change in an article of ours recently shifted our reference from the family becoming a successful, warm "stepfamily" to it becoming a successful, warm "family." Stepfamilies need to know that step relationships can range from very positive to very negative—just as the relationships in real live nuclear families do. Then perhaps, the quality of those step relationships will be less scrutinized and less judged, and therefore become more accepted and positive.

ABUSIVE RELATIONSHIPS

At the present time, physical and sexual child abuse is of great concern because society has become increasingly aware of its prevalence. A recent review of the studies of physical abuse in stepfamilies (Giles-Sims, 1995) points to a lack of agreement regarding abuse in these families. However, using only studies in which the information comes from the reported cases, there is an agreement that children are more at risk of physical abuse in stepfamilies than in nuclear families. Because of the greater complexity of remarriage families, more study is needed to clarify this important issue. For example, there are no studies that indicate the characteristics of the stepfamilies in which the children are at risk for abuse; with the lack of family loyalty in many remarriage families, it may be that abuse is reported more frequently by stepfamily members than it is by members of first-marriage families. In addition, if there is remaining hostility between former spouses or hostility from a stepchild towards a stepparent, unfounded reports of physical abuse may be reported. Finkelhor (1994) reports that a majority of studies do indicate a higher rate in stepfamilies.

This information on physical and sexual abuse suggests that therapists need to be alert to the possibility of child abuse in stepfamilies, but at the same time they need to be cognizant of the added complexity that can surround such an allegation. As an example, in one stepfamily a 15-year-old girl who was angry at her stepfather reported an episode in which he had grabbed her arm during an argument. She reported the he had physically abused her, but since her arm was not red or bruised, the charges, considered spurious, were dropped.

Helping couples form good relationships and enhancing the ability of fathers and stepfathers to nurture their children can help prevent abuse. Treating families in which abuse has occurred or is occurring is a therapeutic area receiving a great deal of attention and is beyond the scope of this book. Special training programs for therapists and agencies devoted to helping abusive families are available in many communities.

CONCLUSION

Not surprisingly, we see a relationship between the eight areas of difficulty discussed in this chapter and the satisfaction of the basic psychological needs included in Chapter 2. As we stated previously, the structure of stepfamilies makes it very difficult, if not impossible, to initially satisfy the three basic needs: to be appreciated and loved, to belong, and to have control over one's life. Many of the challenges to meeting these needs lie in the areas of difficulty outlined in this chapter. Thus, dealing successfully with these areas can provide a good foundation for meeting those basic needs. The following connections make clear the relationships between the content of this chapter and the important psychological needs mentioned above:

Unrealistic beliefs are common to most new stepfamilies. They permeate the thinking and lead to considerable distress because the beliefs have to do with expectations that the basic psychological needs will be adequately met within a short time, that is, there will be almost instant caring and appreciation between stepfamily members and that things will settle down and be under control relatively quickly.

The other areas of difficulty each relate more specifically to one specific need:

1. *Changes and losses, loyalty conflicts, life-cycle discrepancies*, and *closeness and distance* are all concerned with loss or loss of important relations, and carry within them the desire to be understood, appreciated, and loved.

2. Being an *insider or outsider* is intimately connected to the need to belong.
3. *Power issues* and *boundary problems* are closely
   related to the need to have control over important
   situations in one's life.

Many of the concerns that bring stepfamily members
into therapy are related to the difficulties described throughout this chapter. Recognizing these concerns as difficulties in satisfying basic emotional needs can be very useful
for family members because it can help them to understand the source of their discomfort, learn to empathize
with one another, and find creative ways to deal with the
many challenges in their stepfamily life.

5

INTERVENTIONS

This chapter is concerned with a number of specific interventions that are especially useful in therapy with stepfamilies. In a detailed analysis of the therapy research project outlined in Chapter 1, respondents mentioned all of the interventions included here except a few, such as reframing or enhancing self-esteem, that might not be recognized as such by clients. The most acknowledged interventions are validation, normalization, strengthening the couple relationship, psychoeducation, and reduction of helplessness. The first two interventions are discussed under the headings "Enhance Self-Esteem," "Assist with Recognition and Acceptance of Losses," and "Clarify Realistic Expectations." The following three interventions are discussed under their own headings. While other families also appear in some examples, the Cohen family genogram (Exhibit 5.1) is given here because many vignettes refer to this particular stepfamily.

At the time this genogram was drawn, Ruth and Joshua had been married for two years. Joshua and his former wife Ellen had been married for 17 years, from 1973 to 1990, and after their divorce, their children, Jenny and Phil, lived most of the time with Ellen, spending two weekends a month with Joshua. (In our genograms, the solidity of the lines around adults and children indicates the amount of time they are together.) Ruth's first husband, Joe, died in 1989 after they had been married for 14 years. Ruth's children, Sara, John, and Lisa, have always lived full time with their mother.

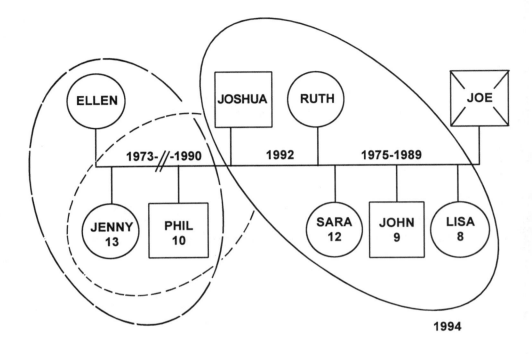

ELLEN JOSHUA RUTH JOE

1973-//-1990 1992 1975-1989

JENNY 13 PHIL 10 SARA 12 JOHN 9 LISA 8

1994

Exhibit 5.1. The Cohen Family.

The parents and siblings of both Joshua and Ruth live more than 2000 miles away from the couple, and a simplified genogram is given here to clarify the relationships between the individuals referred to in the vignettes throughout this chapter.

Although the couple had been married for two years, their household was still chaotic much of the time. Ruth felt she was to blame for the tension and Joshua was happy to have her take that responsibility. Ruth was the one to call a therapist, and after she had one or two visits alone, Joshua came to most sessions with her. When the couple began working fairly well as a team, the children were included in a few appointments. At no time was Ellen willing to talk with a counselor. As with many remarried families who enter therapy because they become stuck in their process toward satisfactory integration, the support and knowledge the Cohen family gained in therapy enabled them to settle down and continue to progress. Throughout this chapter when the Cohen family is used as an example, you may need to refer back to this genogram, although in general the vignettes are self-explanatory.

1. ENHANCE SELF-ESTEEM

The importance of therapeutic acceptance and support is illustrated by the words of a stepmother of three whose therapist unfortunately could not give her the understanding she needed. She wrote:

> I had been married for five years, and I have no children of my own, but I do have three teenage stepchildren. I was a professional person, and then all of a sudden I couldn't cope. I've seen a therapist now for seven months, and I even was in the hospital for awhile. I simply fell apart. Then I read a book about stepfamilies, and in the first 37 pages it validated me. I said, "Wow! I'm not crazy after all!"
>
> I think even good therapists don't know what's going on. I told my therapist that she'd not validated my feelings, and it had made me feel that I was an awful person, a really weak person. She also kept telling me I knew what I was getting into. I showed her the part of the book that said that wasn't true! My sense of identity was all gone. She kept trying to move the family to a nuclear family, and I'm NOT the mother; I'm a parental helper.
>
> I'm going to stay on in therapy for myself, but we need someone who knows about stepfamilies to help our family.

Ruth Cohen is a good example of how therapeutic interaction can increase self-esteem. In therapy, Ruth began to see her new family more realistically and this recognition overcame her depression and feelings of helplessness; she accepted the fact that she alone was not responsible for the functioning of the family. As her self-esteem increased, she no longer considered that something was wrong with her. Previously, Ruth blamed herself for their problems, and her husband Joshua also tended to blame her as a way of bolstering his own self-esteem.

Ruth could now talk with Joshua without anger or self-incrimination, and they began to meet the challenges of the family together.

2. ASSIST WITH RECOGNITION AND ACCEPTANCE OF LOSSES

Therapists need to be alert to explore losses that have gone unrecognized, as well as to give sufficient attention to the conscious losses mentioned by clients. The following discussion adds to the section in Chapter 4 dealing with this major area of difficulty for stepfamilies.

Because the adults have wanted to form their new family unit, they often are unaware of the losses they have sustained in doing so; if they feel sad they believe that it signals that they have a psychological problem. "Getting married makes you happy, so why would I feel so sad ?" one wife asked.

Pertinent information can lead to an exploration of the couple's many losses. For example, a therapist can ask:

a. Have you moved to a new area and house or apartment?
b. With whom were you living before your recent marriage?
c. Who is in your household now?
d. Have you made a job change?
e. Are there other changes in your life that occurred when you got remarried?

To illustrate, Marcie and Charles were married in Albuquerque, New Mexico, because Charles was in the army and had just been transferred there. Marcie and her children had been living in Arizona; Charles and his children were from Texas. All the children came to Albuquerque for the marriage of their parents. However, after a brief glimpse of the couple's new home, Charles's daughter flew back to Texas, and Marcie's two daughters left for Arizona. Each parent had one son remaining to live with them in Albuquerque.

It is not difficult to be aware of some of the couple's major losses: a familiar home; a familiar city with familiar schools, shopping areas, and workplaces; and time together for three of the five parent–child relationships. Some less recognized losses can surface with the need for finding new doctors, dentists, and hairdressers; time alone to unwind; one-on-one time for the couple and for the adults and the children in their household; new friends to talk with; peers the children know in the new neighborhood; and familiar recreational activities.

There are specific losses for children that may not be regarded as significant by the adults:

- The need to now share a bedroom with a sibling or stepsibling
- A change in bedtime
- A change in the type of food served
- A change in ordinal position in the family
- Some loss of connection with a parent
- A shift in roles within the family

Indeed, the adults often believe that a reduction in the amount of responsibility a child can have following a remarriage will be greatly appreciated by the young person. In some situations this may be true, but in many others the children feel "demoted" from a position with greater status that they had held when they were in their parent's single-parent household. Adults often have difficulty understanding the negative aspects of these changes for children. As one new stepfather said, "I hope to help a boy who has lost his status as man of the house return to his rightful role as a growing child."

If teens lose their former "jobs" as confidants or helpers to their parents, the loss is easier if the former role is acknowledged and respected, rewarded, and replaced by a similar or new role welcomed by the adolescent. Sometimes, the family can plan a formal ceremony to accomplish this transfer.

This is an area in which an "award ceremony" can take on special importance for teenagers who have taken on considerable family responsibility during the single-parent household phase. When the single parent remarries, the new spouse may assume most of the role carried earlier by the adolescent. The young person then becomes "unemployed," losing a role that had brought with it a special status and more adult privileges prior to the parent's remarriage, even though it may have been burdensome.

In such instances, adolescents and even younger children may say, "I can't go back to being a child," and clashes with the adults become routine. Early in the marriage, avoiding abrupt changes in the teenager's role can bring a more positive response from the teenager (Gamache, 1993). When role changes must be made, the key to a successful shift seems to be adult acknowledgment and appreciation of the former contribution of the teenager, with all family members present so they are aware of this recognition. A family discussion often follows regarding necessary changes and the working out of satisfactory new roles. At times, therapists help the family actually plan and execute an "Award Ceremony" for the "retiree," complete with a tangible "award" that would be appreciated by the teenager (Coale, 1993).

After a remarriage, some adults are aware that they miss many warm and positive times they had in their previous marriage before it became troubled, but usually most remarried adults are more preoccupied with the negative aspects of the former relationship. As a result, awareness of the losses connected with the erosion of first-marriage dreams and the ending of warm previous family moments does not surface until later in a remarriage. In many new stepfamilies, this delay may be appropriate. For others, where this type of unrecognized loss may be causing a lack of commitment to the present partner or family, mourning of this part of the past may be necessary. Raising these issues in an individual session is advisable unless there has been sufficient time for the new couple to have a truly solid foundation to their relationship. Having a partner of two years listen to the other's poignant memories of a previous 12-year marriage may not be productive!

3. CLARIFY REALISTIC EXPECTATIONS

There are a number of myths that seem believable to many stepfamily adults when they form a stepfamily. The most important have been addressed in Chapter 4, namely:

a. The initial family chaos will settle down quickly.
b. Stepparents and stepchildren will care deeply about one another almost immediately.
c. Stepfamilies can be the same as nuclear families.

In one form or another, these and other unrealistic expectations need to be examined in therapy since the discrepancy between reality and unrealistic expectations usually leads to depression and anger. In one stepfamily panel consisting of five men, each of them spoke of expecting his stepfamily to settle down very quickly. One even admitted that his time limit had originally been two weeks! For two of these men, therapy had been a helpful, though sobering, experience. Letting go of these unrealistic expectations often leads to depression and anger, as Ruth illustrates during several individual session, with the therapist:

Therapist: You seem very angry today.
Ruth: Yes, I am.
Therapist: I'm not sure what your anger is about.

> *Ruth:* You told us that stepfamilies have some
> characteristics different from original families,
> and they will never be the same as original
> families. This makes me very angry because I
> saw this marriage as a second chance to have a
> perfect family. When I grew up, I was pretty
> unhappy with my own family, but I always held
> my aunt's family as the model I wanted when I
> had my own family. My first marriage wasn't so
> hot, and now you're telling me I can't use my
> aunt's family as a model any more.

Part of Ruth's anxiety and low self-esteem when she
came into family therapy had been related to her continued attempts to be "supermom." She saw therapy as a way
to a forge good stepmother relationship with her stepchildren and so as not to be seen as a "wicked stepmother." Her
efforts were rejected by her 13-year-old stepdaughter,
Jenny, and Ruth had blamed herself. Using her aunt as a
model, she had tried even harder to be a "perfect mother."
To her dismay, there seemed to be more, rather than less,
family tension. At this point, she saw the therapist's
comments about stepfamily dynamics as a rejection of the
type of family she was attempting to create. Instead of
feeling better about herself, Ruth felt depressed because
she no longer could feel that her actions would create the
model family she had hoped for.

The therapist continued to see the adults individually
for several appointments. During this period, he made it
clear to Ruth that he understood her anger, and Ruth was
then able to acknowledge the depression that lay beneath
her anger. Slowly, she was able to let go of her unrealistic
expectations of herself and others in the family. She relaxed and did not try to push for a positive relationship with
Jenny. In a joint session with her husband somewhat later,
Ruth admitted with some surprise that the household
seemed more relaxed, "...and Jenny and I are really beginning to get along. It's wonderful!" Joshua supported his

wife's perceptions and complimented her on her willingness to back off and not attempt to rush into closeness with
the children. The Cohen family needed help to work out
other areas of concern, but Ruth's acceptance of more
realistic expectations of herself and her family helped to lay
a more solid foundation upon which all of them could build.

4. STRENGTHEN THE COUPLE RELATIONSHIP

In first-marriage families, having children tends to hold
families together even if the couple's relationship is less
than satisfactory. In a remarriage, the opposite is true—the
presence of children acts to separate rather than keep
unsatisfied couples together (White & Booth, 1985). We
think this is not difficult to understand. In stepfamilies,
there are strong preexisting alliances between parents and
children, and returning to a calmer single-parent household can seem like a desirable alternative. If children are
unhappy in the remarriage, parents' feelings of guilt or
loyalty to their children can pull a couple apart. Therefore,
for the stability of the stepfamily it is essential that the
couple develop a warm and satisfying relationship.

Research indicates that the best predictor of stepfamily
happiness is the relationship between the stepparent and
stepchild (Crosbie-Burnett, 1984). However, without a
solid couple relationship, good steprelationships are not
likely to have the opportunity to develop, and family
chaos does not subside.

All well-functioning families need a couple capable of
creating a parenting team to deal with family issues. In a
remarriage family, forming this team can be difficult because, from the very first, there are many competing tasks.
As a result, couples often neglect to nourish their own
relationship because they are trying to meet everyone's
needs and move towards full family integration. Couples
may need therapy or a stepfamily support group to give
them an understanding that the children need them to

make a commitment to their own relationship. Without it, the whole family has little chance of surviving.

When stepfamily couples who had been in therapy were asked, "What was the single most important factor, whether or not related to therapy, that brought stability to your family?" over 25% of respondents gave a similar response: that making a commitment to their relationship was what helped the most. For example, they would write things like, "The husband and wife relationship comes first, and we stand as a team"; "Balancing family time with couple time"; "Closeness with husband. The marriage relationship comes first"; or, "A thorough commitment to our couple relationship is first and foremost." (See research study, Chapter 1.)

How does a therapist help a couple to strengthen their relationship? The following suggestions can help:

  a. See the couple alone, without the children. Often this is the first opportunity the couple have had for the two of them to work together on couple or family matters.
  b. Be clear that the new couple is *the* couple in the household now. They have a primary long-term relationship that hopefully, will outlast the period when parent–child relationships are predominant. Children will grow up and become independent as they become mature and form their own families.
  c. A solid couple relationship is necessary to prevent another divorce and painful loss of a family for the children.
  d. Help the couple to communicate with one another, so that they will better understand each other and be better able to empathize with each other.
  e. Let couples know that it is important for them to make a place in their lives to be alone in order to nourish their relationship.
  f. Point out that the couple relationship is a model

for the children as they form their own relationships.

When the Cohen family came for therapy, the therapist
saw Ruth and Joshua as a couple for most of their appointments during the first three months. Ruth was feeling
overwhelmed and inadequate, and Joshua had begun to
criticize her interactions with his children. The therapist
discovered that the couple had not been away from their
children for more than three hours at a time during the two
years of their marriage; even these brief periods occurred
infrequently.

Particularly difficult times for Ruth were the weekends
and vacation periods when Phil and Jenny were with them.
As she put it, "I simply lose Joshua during those times."
With a nudge from their therapist, Joshua and Ruth planned
a special evening for themselves before Ruth's stepchildren were with them, and during vacation times the couple
planned to have at least one weekend for themselves.
Having a special time of closeness resulted in Ruth feeling
more secure in her relationship to her husband and finding
her resentment of her stepchildren's relationship to their
father melting away. Joshua relaxed, and his criticism
diminished. With replenished inner "emotional reser-
voirs," the adults had a great deal more emotional and
physical energy, and stepfamily times became a source of
pleasure instead of frustration.

5. PROVIDE PSYCHOEDUCATION

Many stepfamily adults who seek therapy have given little
consideration to the emotional and behavioral implications of living in such a complex family system. As a
result, a primary therapeutic need may be for factual
information from the therapist. Indeed, the stepfamily
couples responding to the stepfamily therapy research
study previously discussed listed educational information

as one of the most positive aspects of their therapy. Conversely, the therapist's lack of knowledge of stepfamily issues was the most frequently cited negative aspect of therapy.

When therapists have little knowledge of stepfamily issues and dynamics, they may have difficulty building a trusting relationship with their stepfamily clients, and they may be less able to normalize typical emotions and situations. This is an important lack, since normative information, changes in clients' perceptions, and exploration of ways in which to handle common stepfamily difficulties can be the basis for therapeutic interactions in stepfamily therapy.

Information about stepfamily tasks and norms is given throughout this book, and Exhibit 2.1 (on pages 23–27) provides many suggestions in outline form that are the result of clinical observation or of empirical research that help with the lengthy integration process. Because they are of major importance in stepfamilies, three areas where education is especially important are discussed in this section: stepparent roles, remarried parent roles, and the need for dyadic relationships within the family unit.

A. Stepparent Roles

Research has shown that there are many satisfactory roles for stepparents in relation to their stepchildren, including mentor, confidante, adult friend, or an additional parenting individual (Crosbie-Burnett, 1984; Mills, 1984). And, in a stepparent–stepchild relationship, the needs of the children as well as the wishes of the stepparent are of primary importance. However, these cannot be considered separately from the wishes of the remarried parent in the stepfamily household and the influence of the divorced parent, who is living elsewhere. Even a deceased parent can exert an influence through what the remarrying parent or children assume that person "would have wanted." Basically, then, the role of stepparents depends on four interacting elements:

- The wishes and needs of the children
- The wishes of the divorced parent in another household
- The expectations and needs of the partner of the stepparent
- The needs of the stepparent (Hetherington, 1989).

No wonder there can be confusion and lack of clarity!

Fortunately, research has clarified several important elements in satisfactory stepparent–stepchild relationships (Kurdek & Fine, 1993). The first of these is the need for the stepparent to slowly work his or her way into the family. The remarried parent has the authority as far as the children are concerned, while the stepparent has to earn the children's respect, and this takes time. A satisfactory relationship is the first requirement, and even with young children it can take one to one and a half or two years for a relationship to form (Stern, 1978). From the first, it is important for the stepparent to support the parent's role with the children. Children become upset if they feel that their stepparent is attempting to replace a parent; with adolescents, though, stepparents may come into the family too late to take on a parenting role. However, stepparents can play important roles in a teenager's life. Frequently, teens will say, "I can talk to my stepparent and say things I can't tell my parents because my parents are too close to me and would get upset."

In some stepfamilies, of course, the differences between stepparents and stepchildren are so great that the best they can do is just "get along" until the children are grown and living on their own.

B. Role of the Remarried Parent

Remarried parents need to take a very different role in the family. Unfortunately, as we have mentioned, they frequently have two expectations that can be detrimental to the integration of the stepfamily. The first is the expectation that the stepparent can take on an authoritative position with the stepchildren; the second is the expectation that the stepparent and the stepchildren will love one another almost immediately. During the single-parent household phase, the parent may have wished to escape taking on a disciplinarian role with the children, and with a remarriage the parent often relinquishes the authoritative parenting role entirely and attempts to turn it over to the new stepparent. However, stepparents cannot initially take on this role, since biological parents are usually the only ones with a close enough relationship with their children to take on a disciplinary role with them. Both research and clinical observation support the necessity for the remarried parent to take an active authoritative parenting role and underline the importance of the stepparent supporting the parenting done by the remarried parent.

Discipline was an important element of therapy for the Cohen family. The following vignette is a session in which the adults saw the value of trying a new organization within the family:

Joshua and Ruth had never worked out a satisfactory way of handling day-to-day family discipline situations. Joshua expected to wield the power in the household, and Ruth was happy with her husband's perception of his role. Ruth had grown up in a family in which her father disciplined her and her brother, and in her first marriage her husband, Joe, had been the disciplinarian. After her husband died, Ruth had been unable to control the children, and she had looked forward to having Joshua become the disciplinarian. After two years of marriage, however, the household was still chaotic. Angry and vituperative episodes often took place between the two adults, the adults and the children, or the children themselves.

Not unexpectedly, the topic of house rules and limit setting was raised by the couple during their first therapeutic session. Both Ruth and Joshua spoke about their concern for their own children and their frustration with their stepchildren. In answer to the therapist's questions, they also acknowledged anger at one another.

While Ruth felt it was suitable for Joshua to discipline her children, she was upset at the way he did it. She felt he was always angry at them and was much too strict. On the other hand, Joshua felt that his wife "babied" her children and resented his two children whenever they were around. When the therapist asked about the children's reactions, the adults painted a picture of open rebellion on the part of Ruth's children, Sara, John, and Lisa, and episodes of extreme rivalry between the two sets of children. Ruth said, "There are no happy campers in this family!"

The therapist acknowledged the couple's pain and their concern, and complimented them on their ability to speak about such topics with a touch of humor. He also commented that these were difficult yet common situations that frequently arise in families like theirs. He informed Ruth and Joshua that there are many guidelines emerging for handling these problems. He gave them hope that they could make changes and the couple left the session feeling less anxious and depressed, and with the sense that they were understood by the therapist.

The therapist next helped the couple understand how past family history affected them. He discussed the following points:

- Exploration of the family organization in Ruth and Joshua's families of origin, in their first marriages, and in their single-parent households
- Their previous histories of the father being in charge of the household
- Ruth's inability to assume the disciplinarian role in her single-parent household

The therapist called Ruth and Joshua's attention to the models they had used and that had been part of their former family units. He also pointed out that parents most frequently follow the parenting patterns experienced in their families of origin. Although these earlier patterns were acceptable to Joshua and Ruth and had worked to some degree in their first marriages, the therapist explained that a great deal of research indicated that because of the different structure and dynamics in stepfamilies, the authoritative role with the children in these families works better if it is taken on by the children's biological parent. He then talked of the need for stepparents to form a caring relationship with their stepchildren before they slowly take on a disciplinary role.

At this point the following conversation occurred:

Joshua: But this has always been my role.

Ruth: And I'm not good at getting my children to obey me.

Joshua: How could it work anyway? We each have children in the house every weekend. I can't imagine having a bunch of different rules for my children and for Ruth's children.

Therapist: You both are raising good points. Before talking more about them, I have a basic question. Am I correct that you both feel things in this area are not working smoothly in your household?

Couple: (nodding agreement)

Therapist: So would you be willing to make some changes?

Joshua: If Ruth's children would pay attention to what I say, that's all it would take to change everything.

Ruth: I don't think that's fair. My children aren't used to your rules. Besides, I think you're harder on them than you are on Phil and Jenny. No wonder my children are resentful.

This preceding dialogue represents typical responses to such a situation. It usually takes some time for the adults to understand and empathize with their stepchildren's feelings as well as they do with their own children's losses, anger, and fear. As their understanding grew, Joshua and Ruth also began to appreciate their partner's feelings and behavior as well. Finally they began to talk about the need to work together on the house rules, and they began to wonder what it would be like to leave the parenting of each set of children in the hands of their biological parent.

Ruth commented that she would need some help with her parenting skills, but she didn't think having Joshua help her would work. The therapist suggested that the couple take a parenting class together to add to the parenting knowledge that each of them already had, and he made separate appointments with each of them to discuss their individual reactions to his suggestion.

In these individual appointments, each adult began to observe what worked in the family. Joshua began to withdraw from "being the heavy" with Ruth's children, and with the therapist's support, Ruth began to set limits for her children in areas especially troublesome to both adults. After a few joint appointments in which the couple worked productively together, an appointment was made for all the children to join the couple. The therapist helped the children and adults talk to one another, beginning by modeling a "family meeting" in the office to discuss together what was needed for the family to function satisfactorily (preparation of food, marketing, cleaning the house, etc.). The children were delighted to have their input solicited, and Ruth and Joshua were surprised at how valuable their suggestions were.

Remarried parents usually need to "back off" from expecting an instant caring relationship between the stepparent and stepchildren, and this situation was true in the Cohen family. Step relationships take time to develop, and attempting to force them can lead to alienation rather than understanding and bonding. While it takes time for stepparents and stepchildren to get to know one another and to begin to create a satisfactory relationship, the biological parent of the children can help by requiring the children to be respectful of the stepparent. This is important since without this requirement lack of respect or civility within the household can create an environment in which there is little chance for new positive relationships to form.

During several subsequent family sessions the children were challenged to help the adults with other family rule changes, and Ruth and Joshua began requiring the children to be respectful toward their stepparent. In turn, Joshua and Ruth were becoming more supportive of their stepchildren.

Although remarried parents often feel helpless and caught between the needs of their partner and the needs of their children, in actuality they have the most power in the household because they are members of both the couple and the parent–child subsystems. The truth of this soon became clear to Ruth and Joshua, and they realized that they were in a position to help bring the children and their stepparent closer together. In addition, the therapist needed to help the two adults as they created enough space in their relationship with their children for the stepparent–stepchild relationships to form. Gradually, as the interpersonal relationships improved, the household settled down.

C. Dyadic Relationships Within the Family Unit

Special one-on-one times in remarriage families are important. In fact, while this can be a crucial element in developing and maintaining relationships in stepfamilies, one-on-one times are important in all families (Visher, E. B., 1994). This is one of the most important lessons for other families to learn from the experience of stepfamily members who need to protect important parent–child alliances and to build new couple bonds and ties between stepparents and stepchildren, and also between stepsiblings.

There are many references to the importance of the couple relationship. Too often the adults are trying so hard to form a "family" that they forget to take needed individual time for themselves and one-on-one time for the two of them. Waiting for "free time" to be alone does not work for most couples. They need to be encouraged to plan for time together—perhaps taking a walk, going out alone for coffee or a movie, or for more extended times when the children are older. Unfortunately, time together can turn into a discussion of family problems. This not helpful. Couples need the direction to agree *not* to talk about the family during their "special times" together.

Children in stepfamilies frequently express the wish for time alone with a parent. They may have had this exclusive time during the single-parent household phase before the parent's remarriage. Arranging for parent and child to have one-on-one times helps reduce the child's sense of loss that occurs when the parent now has others to relate to. Childen usually want more special time than is possible, but many parents and stepparents do not realize the importance of meeting this need to some degree. As one child said, "I want time alone with my Dad, me and my Dad alone. I don't understand why it always has to be with my stepbrothers and sisters. Why does the *whole family* have to go out?" Getting a book together at the library or playing a computing game together can be very fulfilling for a child.

Sometimes it is difficult for the stepparent who may feel left out at these moments. What can make a difference is for the stepparents to know that time alone with each of their stepchildren is important too. This is what builds new relationships. Not having the parent present can allow the new step relationship to grow as the two plan to do something together that they both will enjoy.

One large stepfamily talked about the need they had discovered for all the children to have special one-on-one

times as well. This family found that without these opportunities, difficulties among the children would begin to
surface.

At times it seems almost magical how much the giving
of undivided attention nourishes interpersonal relationships.

6. REDUCE A SENSE OF HELPLESSNESS

Because stepfamily structure does not meet the need for
control over one's life as well as first marriages do, helping
stepfamily members gain some sense of mastery over their
lives can be an important aspect of therapy.

Legally, custodial parents have greater power than
noncustodial parents as far as their parent–child relationships are concerned. Stepparents have the least power
legally, though the partner of the custodial parent may at
times have more family control than the noncustodial
parent (Visher & Visher, 1988).

While therapy cannot directly change society's impact
in this area, it is important to recognize the anger and
depression that can be caused by external forces. There are
many situations over which stepfamily members feel they
have little control, and in these areas therapy can be
extremely helpful.

Labeling and understanding problems along with information and ideas on ways to cope with them are a major
help in therapy. Understanding and labeling stepfamily
issues allows parents and stepparents to feel more in
control. For example, Joshua felt helpless in his interactions with his former wife, Ellen. The therapist pointed out
the difficulty ex-spouses have working together and explored with Joshua and Ruth ways in which their contact
with Ellen might be more successful. Unfortunately, Ellen
was not able to cooperate and the therapist helped the
couple to recognize that although they could not control

Ellen's household, they need not relinquish the control that they did have. For instance, instead of continuing with their struggle to have Ellen come on time to take Phil and Jenny back home on weekends, Joshua and Ruth arranged to drive the children in both directions. This took more of their time since the children's primary residence was with their mother in a suburb 30 minutes away. However, the emotional relaxation that came from having control over these situations more than compensated for their travels. In addition, the couple often went together and this gave them a little more time alone to relate to one another.

In other families, the residential parent may be the one feeling frustrated and angry because the children's other parent is behaving irresponsibly in coming for or returning the children. If it remains impossible for the two parents to cooperate, the residential parent may need help in determining a satisfactory way to have control in this area.

Children as well may not be taking control in personal areas, or they may not have been given appropriate responsibilities and privileges. In the Cohen family, the therapist helped the adults allow Sara to make her own school lunch so it would be what she wanted, and they let her make her own choices of after-school activities at her middle school. Sara responded to having more control in these areas by growing more active and enthusiastic about going to school, and while the early weekday mornings in the Cohen family remained hectic, the emotional tone changed dramatically.

7. USE GENOGRAMS

Diagramming families is helpful to most families because it helps therapists and family members to visualize the family system. The "supra family system" (Sager, et al., 1983) and the complexity of stepfamily systems make diagrams of particular importance. They often give step-family members a better understanding of why they are feeling overwhelmed, and they can reduce therapists' confusion about the many individuals involved. In addition, genograms give therapists considerable family information and history very quickly. In the case of step-families with their mixture of emotions regarding former spouses, completing a genogram may lead family members to talk about individuals *not* talked about in their family.

The following genogram (Exhibit 5.2) illustrates a complex stepfamily system. It is drawn using the system outlined in McGoldrick and Gerson (1985), with residential information indicated in a way that we find helpful.

The genogram drawn here is more complex than the one for the Cohen family on page 108. However, the symbolic representation is the same, with the additional symbol, here a $\triangle$, which represents a pregnancy. In this family, Don and Sue are the couple who came for therapy. After the genogram was drawn, Sue looked at the complexity of their genogram and said vehemently, "That's what I wanted to talk about!" In another remarriage family, the husband/remarried father looked at the deaths and losses his wife had sustained, then at the rich network on his side of the family, and remarked to his children with sudden understanding, "No wonder Pamela feels left out. She has no one on her side, and we have all these people!"

In a third family, a remarried mother responded to the family understanding she had gained from the genogram of their stepfamily by saying, "That was really, really helpful to see the dynamics of the whole thing. It puts it in a nutshell and makes it more precise. It gives you the big picture." Drawing a genogram when taking a family history can be a very powerful tool for understanding and change. (There are instructions for constructing genograms that include residential information in Visher and Visher, 1988, pp. 33–40.)

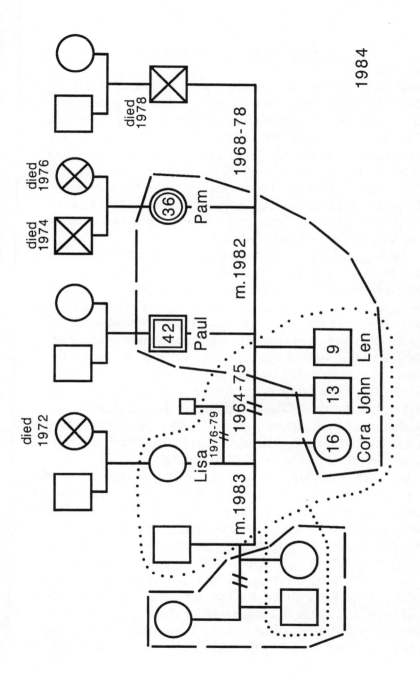

Exhibit 5.2. Sample Genogram.

Reprinted from Visher, E. B. & Visher, J. S., (1988). *Old Loyalties, New Ties: Therapeutic Strategies with Stepfamilies.*
New York: Brunner/Mazel. p. 35.

8. FILL IN PAST HISTORIES

New stepfamilies are families with no family history. Until the individuals have been together for a period of time, there are few shared memories. Adults may have shared some of their past history with one another, but other family members may not have done so. One teenager illustrated this "memory deficit" when he said, "I was eight when my mother remarried, but I can't feel the same about my stepfather as I do about my mother. There were eight years in which I knew my mom, but those years in my stepfather's history are a blank to me."

Taking a family history or inquiring into specific family-events can be a helpful assessment tool with a first-marriage family; with a stepfamily it can be an important therapeutic intervention. In one family, two children, six and nine, in a therapy session with their stepmother, Pam, spoke of being upset and feeling responsible when Pam became depressed, went into her bedroom, and shut the door. Pam responded by saying, "Oh, it has nothing to do with you. I was depressed long before I ever met your father." In their stepfamily one piece of formerly unknown past history transformed a reoccurring family situation from one that caused guilt and stress for the children to one for which they did not feel responsible.

In another stepfamily, the therapist helped the father of a 13-year-old girl, Judy, to share with her his anguish at having to send her to live with his parents for three years following his wife's death. Judy could then begin to understand his action as reflecting his love for her rather than as a rejection of her. In turn, she shared her pain and the events of her life during those three years. Since this interchange took place in the presence of the whole stepfamily, it became clear to all of them why Judy had been angry at her father and had resisted the family's attempts to get to know her better. As Judy's anger subsided, and the need for her to stay with grandparents began to be understood and accepted, she started to respond positively to what her new family had to offer her.

9. RELATE PAST FAMILY EXPERIENCE TO PRESENT SITUATIONS

All of us are affected by previous experiences in our family or, in the case of a remarriage, in our previous families. In stepfamilies, children as well as adults have prior families, and therefore the mixture of anticipations, fears, and expectations is more complex than in first-marriage families. Exposing parts of the past that have been woven into patterns of the present is often a therapeutic necessity.

If the presenting difficulty concerns the couple relationship, there frequently is value in exploring former connections when the couple is being seen together. This helps depersonalize the problem so that understanding and empathy have more opportunity to replace misunderstanding, antagonism, and pain. However, stepfamily structure increases the likelihood of heightened emotional reactions. The following vignettes illustrate the impact of family of origin situations:

Vignette 1

Eileen and Mike had been together a total of nine years. Both had children who lived with them, Eileen's most of the time and Mike's every weekend. A major problem for Eileen, who was used to strict discipline when she was growing up, was Mike's inability to set limits for his daughter when she was with them. Mike explained that when he was young, he did not need parental discipline; rather he hid any misbehavior from his parents because he was afraid of their reaction. He then commented that he found it much easier to discipline his stepson than to set limits for his daughter:

> *Therapist:* Why do you think that is?
>
> *Mike:* I don't know (*long pause*). I guess I'm afraid I might lose some of her love.
>
> *Therapist:* Eileen had the experience of seeing parents who disciplined her and yet they didn't lose her love. I guess you didn't have the experience of seeing parents who disciplined their children and still had a loving relationship with them.
>
> *Mike:* I guess that's right.
>
> *Eileen:* (*leaning forward, with some emotion*) I think I understand why this is so hard for Mike. When Mike was 12, he saw his parents disown his older brother, or at least they said he was dead. (*Tears filled Mike's eyes.*)
>
> *Therapist:* (*nodding*) Yes, no wonder it would be difficult.
>
> (*Eileen's anger melted. She reached out for Mike's hand and they held hands for most of the rest of the session.*)

Vignette 2

Bob and Patsy had been married for four years, and Patsy was very unhappy because she felt Bob cared more for his son than he did for her. This produced continual stress since Bob's son lived with them most of the time.

> *Therapist:* (*to couple*) I wonder what type of relationship your parents had when you were growing up.
>
> *Patsy:* My parents loved each other a lot. They

had fights sometimes, but they didn't last long. They were very affectionate with each other.

Therapist: So you had the model of a couple that cared about each other.

Patsy: Yes.

Bob: I didn't have that. My parents fought a lot, and then they divorced each other when I was 10. I lived with my mother, and I saw my dad a couple of times a month.

Therapist: Did your parents remarry?

Bob: My dad did after a few years, but my mother never did.

Therapist: So you and your mother lived together, just the two of you?

Bob: Yes, we were very close. I got along well with her.

Therapist: So your model was a good parent— child relationship and you didn't experience a good couple relationship.

Bob: Yeah. I'd never thought about that.

After this session, in which each recognized the difference in the models they had experienced growing up, there was much greater understanding between them. Bob realized he was repeating the parent-child relationship that had been his and his mother's pattern, and he saw the steps he needed to take to form a stronger union with Patsy. This was easier for him to do as she became less critical as a result of her increased understanding, which allowed her to view his behavior more objectively and less as a personal rejection.

In stepfamilies, children from previous relationships come into the new family with experiences from former families, including the single–parent household phase. Usually, the older they are, the greater the impact these earlier households have on their emotions and behavior in the new family unit. Especially if a divorced or widowed parent has had a series of relationships, children may be reluctant to make an emotional commitment to any new person. And if children have seen their parents arguing and then divorcing, they may become anxious when their parent and stepparent argue because they fear it will lead, as before, to the trauma and upset of another divorce. For 14-year-old Ronda, it was a different story:

Ronda's mother Louise had remarried a divorced man, David, who had three older children who were already living independently. Ronda, age 14, lived full time with her mother and David. She did not see her father because he had disappeared and no one knew where he was living. One day, Louise, David, and Ronda were going out for dinner. Unexpectedly, Ronda became hysterical. She threw things around her room, wouldn't talk to her mother, and lashed out verbally at both of the adults. David, Ronda's stepfather, quietly went into her bedroom and sat in a chair. Ronda broke a glass and crushed it on the floor with her foot. Ronda told him to leave, but David said, "No, I think you need me here." She kept telling him to leave, but he just sat quietly.

Slowly Ronda calmed down, and she and David and Louise were able to talk. The adults had never seen Ronda behave in this manner before and asked her what had been wrong. Ronda asked David why he had stayed when she'd told him to leave. David said, "I was afraid you might hurt yourself. I love you very much and I don't want anything to happen to you. I thought you really needed me here. Your behavior is not going to drive me away. I'm here to stay."

Ronda began to cry and said that she wanted to act "awful" so David would go away and leave her the way her father had done. As a result of her experience with her father, Ronda could not tolerate warm feelings for David because of her fear that he also would leave the way her father had. She wanted to *make* it happen rather than have it happen to her. Gradually, she began to believe that David was not going to go away no matter how she behaved, and from then on she began to relax. Following this event, Ronda and David slowly developed a warm and loving relationship.

Exploring childhood memories or experiences in former family households is useful when the therapist helps the individual go beyond those earlier experiences by linking them appropriately to the present situations that are causing difficulty. One client said to his therapist, "I don't want to spend my time mucking around in the past." However, the past is not the end of the dialogue; rather it can be an important bridge to understanding and altering the present. We see these as important words. The past can be an important bridge to *understanding* and *altering* the present; however, it is only the beginning of the discussion, not the end of the dialogue.

10. MAKE SPECIFIC SUGGESTIONS

The therapy research mentioned in Chapter 1 indicated that stepfamilies do not seek therapy to enhance their growth. Rather, they enter therapy at a time when there is considerable tension and stress within the family and the adults are anxious and depressed because of the turmoil.

As a rule, anxiety and depression reduce an individual's ability to think through problematic situations and work out productive solutions. Offering creative and appropriate suggestions can help reduce anxiety and act as a model for dealing with other difficulties.

In the Cohen family, for example, 13-year-old Jenny was moody and rude when she returned to the home

of her father and stepmother after a weekend with her
mother. Her behavior upset her father, Joshua, and
her stepmother, Ruth, and they began to feel angry
with Jenny's mother. When they pushed Jenny to tell
them what went on during her visits there, Jenny was
even more upset the next time she returned from a
weekend with her mother.

In talking with the couple, the therapist learned that
they expected Joshua's daughter to relate easily and
comfortably with them immediately upon her return
from being with her mother. As well as calling their
attention to the fact that sudden transitions are difficult, the therapist made several specific suggestions
that he considered might help the situation: Greet
Jenny warmly and then suggest that she might like to
roller skate for a few minutes or watch a bit of a
favorite video with them. These were activities Jenny
enjoyed, and she responded positively to these suggestions. Now she could enter the household gradually. The removal of the pressure on Jenny enabled
her to relax and join her father and stepmother when
she felt comfortable. Ruth and Joshua also stopped
asking Jenny about the other household. Instead they
told her about what had happened with them while
she was away. The couple began to realize that they
had been developing negative assumptions about
Jenny's mother's household, but it was they who had
been helping to create the difficulty. When other
touchy situations arose, they found themselves less
emotionally reactive and better able to figure out
satisfactory solutions to problems.

11. SUGGEST HELPFUL RITUALS

Ceremonial rituals such as bar and bat mitzvahs and
weddings are important family events. No less important
in contributing to the sense of family membership are the

daily, more ordinary rituals and ways of doing things: The
seven-year-old sets the table for dinner and the teenagers
take turns cleaning up after the meal; chores are posted on
the refrigerator every Monday; the husband shops and the
wife does the cooking; the family goes out for pizza on
Friday; every other weekend the children go to their other
household. These and many other routine family life
segments form a familiar pattern that provides structure
and predictability for the family.

When stepfamily members first live together, no such
familiarity exists. In one new stepfamily, each of the
adults had enjoyed a previous pattern of doing the marketing and the food preparation. In another, the wife did not
expect the children to help with household chores, while
her husband had relied on his children to take considerable household responsibility. Helping these families
compromise and work out satisfactory new daily routines
became an important therapeutic task. Therapists may
also be called upon to assist stepfamilies in talking together about the celebration of special events that have
held emotional importance for them in the past. For some
it may be Christmas or Thanksgiving rituals, while for
others it may be Sunday supper or the celebration of the
Fourth of July. Special ceremonies in stepfamilies are
important in order to acknowledge family changes and to
mark special times in the life of the new family unit.

12. SEPARATE FEELINGS AND BEHAVIOR

Throughout life we separate feelings from behavior when
our feelings would disrupt our relationships with other
people. In stepfamilies, perhaps because they are so conscious of their emotions and their behavior, many adults
find themselves in conflict in this area, saying, "It would
be hypocritical to act differently than I feel." However,
initially in this type of family there is no "middle ground"
in a Gestalt sense, no solid foundation to many of the

relationships. Therefore, until this foundation has time to develop, it is often necessary to separate behavior from feelings so that there is no disruption to a developing relationship. It can be critical, not hypocritical, to do so:

Joshua had been away for two weeks on a business trip. On his return, he greeted his 10-year-old son, Phil, warmly, and presented him with an intriguing metal truck that flashed its lights and gave warning signals when it reversed its course. His greeting to his nine-year-old stepson John was strained and his present was a plastic flute that could be used to play a tune if you were skilled. The nine-year-old ran to his mother, Ruth, in tears, which increased the distress she had already felt as she watched her husband's interactions with the two boys.

In therapy Joshua talked about the difference in his feelings for his son and for his stepson. To him it did not seem "right" to bring the boys presents of equal importance when he did not have "equal" feelings for them. However, Joshua was concerned about the continuing upset in the family and began to see the necessity of changing his behavior so as to promote the growth of his relationship with his stepson. He realized he had no difficulty separating his behavior and his feelings in business situations. For example, he had sent a memo to his boss asking to talk with him about a matter that had angered him, rather than writing him a scathing note that would have more accurately matched his feelings. Joshua began to understand how much more crucial such behavior was in his new family, and he took both the boys to the zoo and bought each one a desired toy in the gift shop while they were there. Not only did his stepson respond happily, but his wife was pleased when the three of them returned home from the outing.

In another family, in which there was ongoing hostility between 14-year-old Timothy and his stepmother, Gwen,

Gwen's therapist suggested that for two weeks Gwen act towards Timothy "as if" he really liked her and she really liked him. Gwen tried this and her altered behavior set in motion a positive interactional pattern between them. Timothy responded to the change in Gwen's behavior by becoming less combative and more talkative, and their relationship began to improve.

Even when situations remain tense and awkward, stepparents need to try to be "fair" in their dealings with the children and parents need to require civility in the relationships in the household. This can help everyone live together more smoothly so that better relationships have an opportunity to develop.

Grandparents are often guilty of showing favoritism towards their biological grandchildren, leaving out their stepgrandchildren. This tends to occur because the biological grandchildren have had a long-term relationship with their grandparents and the stepgrandchildren have not. The tension caused by such a circumstance can often be resolved by a suggestion that the remarried parent talk to his/her parents and gently inform them that their lack of fairness, lack of acceptance of a new spouse, or failure to recognize that there is a new family in the picture is causing difficulty in the household. Often, it is enough simply to draw the attention of the grandparents to this situation and they will change their behavior towards new family members. When grandparents do not make the necessary changes, it may be desirable to include them in family therapy sessions. The situation with Jerry and his parents illustrates how a remarried "child" had to take a strong position with his parents:

> Even though Jerry and Karen had been married for two years, Jerry's parents would have nothing to do with Karen. Karen had no children, and Jerry's son was their only grandchild. Jerry and his son, Freddy, continued to see Jerry's parents without Karen.
>
> Jerry talked with his parents, but they continued to refuse to have any contact with Karen. Eventually,

Jerry had to let his parents know that this arrangement
was hurting him a great deal and was not acceptable to
him. Jerry told his parents that he loved them, but that
he could not continue to bring their grandson to see
them (when Freddy was visiting Jerry and Karen)
unless Karen came too.

After a period of four or five months, Jerry's parents
agreed to include Karen. To ease into the situation,
their first time together was for dinner in a restaurant.
Within a year and a half, Freddy and the four adults all
enjoyed each other's company. The adults did things
together frequently, and Freddy visited with his grandparents whenever he was in the area.

13. TEACH NEGOTIATION

Being in a stepfamily requires negotiation skills beyond
the usual. In these families, virtual strangers, adults and
children, come together under one roof with very different ways of thinking, communicating, and behaving. As
a rule, everyone feels displaced initially and out of
control. Marie loves to have her dog, Mitzi, snuggle up
to her when she's sleeping, and she feeds her table scraps
when she and her children are eating. In contrast, her
new husband, Bill, has been living in an apartment where
no pets are permitted and also he is allergic to cat and
dog hair. Marie's children also love Mitzi, while Bill's
children's only pet has been a large turtle and they are
uncomfortable with dogs of any size. As with most things,
there is no right or wrong opinion about pets and, within
reasonable parameters, no right or wrong about how they
are cared for. However, given the differences in these
emotional patterns and ways of living, and Bill's allergy
to cat and dog hair, it is likely that arriving at an emotionally satisfactory solution to the question of Mitzi will be
very difficult.

When Ruth and Joshua Cohen entered therapy, food was an especially thorny area for them. Joshua was used to eating out in fast food restaurants or heating a prepared dinner or a can of beans in his microwave. When his children were with him, they enjoyed going to McDonalds or Pizza Hut. Ruth, on the other hand, had repeated her mother's pattern of cooking most things "from scratch" and using ingredients that conformed to the current information about healthy diets. Joshua considered Ruth a "health nut," while Ruth harbored a deep fear that the high-fat food that Joshua ate would shorten his life significantly.

Joshua was used to being in charge, while Ruth had grown accustomed to deciding by herself what she and her children would eat. At times, Ruth's children would beg (usually unsuccessfully) for some candy or a doughnut, but for the most part they accepted their mother's "health meals" and satisfied their wish for something sweet when she wasn't present.

Helping Ruth and Joshua learn to negotiate became an important therapeutic task. Since food is of primary importance, their lack of agreement in this area became a meaningful topic to be used as the content for their discussion of the negotiation process.

With their therapist's help, Ruth and Joshua slowly moved towards each other's positions in their negotiation process. In their family the following decisions were reached in the solution of their nutritional dilemmas:

1. Different family members would be in charge of choosing the menu for certain days of the week. Since Ruth's children were familiar with her cooking preferences, she was content with their weekly choices.
2. Joshua's children were thrilled to be able to

       choose their meals when they were with their
       father and stepmother, and they accepted a list
       of restaurants on the adults' approved list.

3.   Joshua could choose the menu once a week and
       he found that he had grown to appreciate a
       more leisurely meal than he had been used to
       when he was living alone most of the time. He
       also was finding that he liked many of Ruth's
       recipes.

4.   While Ruth continued to do the cooking, Joshua
       did much of the marketing, and together the
       whole family cleaned the kitchen and washed
       dishes after dinner.

5.   Ruth had become aware that she leaned heavily
       towards forbidding any kind of sweets because
       she had grown up with a father who was dia-
       betic. She relaxed about this, and the children
       no longer found it necessary to sneak candy
       behind her back.

In an emotionally laden area of family interaction,
successful negotiation of the diverse preferences of this
family was an important step forward toward family integration. Helping stepfamily members state their needs,
accept their validity when they differed, and work out
satisfactory solutions through negotiation is essential for
stepfamily happiness. Mastering these skills of negotiation not only benefits the household, but also it is valuable
in a variety of settings outside the family milieu and is
certainly an asset that can emerge from the necessity for
compromise when living in this more complex type of
family.

14. RESTRUCTURE AND REFRAME

Attitudinal studies illustrate that it is the perception of an
event rather than the event itself that determines the

influence on the individual of what has taken place. Unfortunately, society perceives divorce, remarriage, and stepfamily life in less than glowing terms, and this social rejection influences the way in which stepfamily members view many events that take place in their family. For this reason, positive reframing of stepfamily situations can be of particular importance in stepfamily therapy. The Cohen family also illustrates this point:

Joshua and Ruth had been together for two years when they came to talk with the therapist. The couple began working well together, but Joshua's two children continued to be ill at ease in the new family unit, even though they appeared to relate well to Ruth's three children. What was particularly upsetting to the adults was Phil's and Jenny's repeated wish to have time alone with their father, Joshua. The couple interpreted this as the children's attempt to separate them and they refused to pay attention to the children's requests.

The therapist reframed the wish in a positive manner by calling attention to Joshua's children's need to reduce their sense of loss. They wished some time alone with Joshua similar to the exclusive relationship they had enjoyed with him after the divorce of Joshua and their mother. Joshua and Ruth were able to understand this way of thinking about these requests. They recognized that Ruth's children had times alone with their mother and that Joshua's children did not have times together with their father without Ruth or the other children being present. While the adults continued to plan special family times, they also made sure that Joshua had time to help Jenny with her homework or to play Nintendo games with Phil, things Joshua had done before his remarriage. Ruth also built her relationship with her stepchildren by taking them for ice cream alone or shopping from time to time with Jenny. Now that they felt more "special," and even though they would have liked to have more one-on-one time with their father, Phil and Jenny appreciated the time they had and the family relationships improved.

In another family, Joan, the stepmother of 13-year-old Mary, was upset that Mary often openly rejected her and she felt that Mary disliked her. In talking with their therapist, Joan and her husband, Jason, spoke at some length about Mary's close relationship with her biological mother with whom she lived most of the time. Mary was with Joan and Jason every other weekend.

The couple had hoped that Mary would enjoy their home, which was more relaxed than her mother's. They viewed Mary's mother, Cecilia, as an emotionally intense parent who had a "disorganized" lifestyle. When the therapist wondered aloud if Cecilia might be feeling some insecurity in her relationship with her daughter, Joan and Jason both said they thought this was the case. The therapist then said:

> I suspect that Mary recognizes the psychological differences between Joan and her mother. In fact, she may be wishing that her mother was more like Joan. If so, it may be that Mary really appreciates Joan and likes her, but is pushing her away because she is trying to maintain a close relationship with her mother. If you think of it that way, Joan, you may be able to relax and the two of you can let Mary know that parents and stepparents can have many important characteristics that are different, yet equally valuable. This might help ease the situation.

Jason agreed that Mary basically liked Joan, and Joan agreed to think about it. Slowly Joan began to believe that the therapist was correct, and she responded to Mary with less emotion. Reframing the interaction between Mary and Joan allowed Joan to experience Mary's negativity less personally. When Joan had less need to push for acceptance from her stepdaughter, Mary became less hostile. As Mary matured and recognized that Joan was not competing with her mother, the two began to develop a warm relationship.

15. USE ACCURATE LANGUAGE

It is often difficult for therapists to use accurate language when working with stepfamily individuals because they so often think in nuclear family terms, for example saying "new father" rather than "stepfather" and "new mother" rather than "stepmother." Children can be particularly upset by this if it appears to them that the therapist considers the new person in the family as a replacement for their parent of the same sex. Following the lead of family members is important unless their words require discussion because they do not reflect the present situation. For example, adults may not acknowledge step-relationships in an unconscious attempt to recreate a nuclear family situation. Frequently, a discussion of this behavior reveals that the adults believe that step-relationships cannot be characterized by love and caring. Retaining this belief does little to facilitate the formation of a successful stepfamily!

In an initial interview with a family, the therapist initiated contact with a child by asking, "What do you call your stepparent?" The child responded by giving the stepparent's first name. The therapist subsequently used the same designation. The nomenclature used in remarriage families is more varied than in first-marriage families, and words can be associated with tense emotional reactions. It is dangerous to make assumptions and inaccurate to use nuclear family nomenclature without input from the family.

16. REDUCE THERAPEUTIC TENSION

There are times in therapy with first-marriage families that family members appear to be stuck in unproductive patterns that continue with the family members using little energy to make any interactional shift. At such times, therapists may deliberately intervene in a way to cause more tension in the family so as to motivate family members to explore new solutions. In any remarriage families, however, the opposite type of intervention is necessary. The more usual need is for the therapist to try to reduce the family's tension, thus allowing them to gain sufficient equilibrium to find ways of reducing unacceptable family tensions.

When the chaos in the family continues into the therapy session, the following suggestions may be helpful for reducing the tension:

A. Instead of encouraging direct interaction between family members, especially if there is a lot of anger, suggest that communication go through the therapist. This allows the therapist to interpret or reframe what is being said in a less destructive way. For example, when a mother says to the therapist, "I'm sick and tired of the way my husband treats my children," the therapist can defuse the situation by saying to the husband and stepfather, "I hear your wife saying that it hurts her that you and her children are not getting along together. She loves all of you and this is very upsetting to her."

B. It may be that individuals need to have individual sessions so that their needs can be met more adequately and their anxiety and distress can be reduced.

Hal and Dee needed individual appointments. Their self-esteem was very low and they each needed considerable support from the therapist. They could not empathize or support one another. From time to time they were seen together, alternating with three to four individual appointments for each of them. The therapist consciously chose to see each of them for the same number of individual appointments in order to reduce the opportunity for either one to feel responsible for all the difficulties or to give that responsibility to the spouse. A few times one spouse was seen more than the other when both agreed that one of them could benefit from extra time to explore a particular issue that was causing personal difficulty.

As Hal and Dee gained self-esteem, they were able to be more supportive of one another and to work together on familial difficulties. Gradually, their joint sessions increased in frequency as the need for individual sessions disappeared.

C. With permission, use a tape recorder during therapy sessions. At times, it is helpful to replay and discuss a section of the tape during the hour. At other times, the couple may wish to borrow the tape to listen to it at home. With the tape recorder in sight and running during the session, it acts as an "outsider," with the conversation seeming to go beyond those present. Often, this technique acts as a necessary "governor" for the couple or family interactions.

D. The most effective way of becoming an observer of yourself is to watch yourself on videotape. When it is possible to make this type of a record, it can lead to many positive changes. Emotions and actions that feel a certain way to the person experiencing them can look and feel quite different to another person. A videotape recording allows each person to experience, at least to some extent,

the impact of his or her behavior on others. It can
be an invaluable tool in some situations.

SUMMARY

This chapter reviews 16 specific therapeutic interventions
that have been especially helpful in working with
stepfamilies. No matter which theoretical approach a therapist uses, these suggestions can be useful. The important
thing is to help stepfamily members begin to feel more
comfortable, more hopeful, less helpless than before, and
to have some understanding that what they have been
experiencing is normal. This may require some therapists
to be more active and more directive then they are with
other clients. With most stepfamilies, this appears to be
necessary so that they may gain hope that things will be
better in the future and be encouraged to "hang in there"
for the long haul and thereby avoid another divorce, with
all its pain.

6

HELPING THE CHILDREN
IN STEPFAMILIES

Remarriages when children are not involved can bring emotional and financial complications that do not arise in first marriages. When either or both of the adults have had children previously, their existence creates the much more complex "supra family system" that we have been describing throughout this book. In fact, the presence of children adds more complexity to the family than some adults are able to handle; as a result, the re-divorce rate is higher in remarriages when children are involved than when the marriage is between adults who have no children (White & Booth, 1984). Even when the children are grown or live elsewhere, their existence can affect the marriage in many ways, from the payment of child support to the heartbreak of cut-off relationships.

Relationships between adults and children have been mentioned in connection with many of the stepfamily dynamics already discussed. This chapter deals specifically with children's dilemmas and reactions and ways in which they can be helped in their efforts to adjust to all the changes in their lives. "Settling in" is a process that takes months, or even years, rather than weeks. Also, with the developmental changes that come as children mature, as in any type of family, family growth can be a challenging and never-ending process.

We find it helpful to think of the major issues, regarding

their stepfamily, for stepchildren of any age in terms of the "Three L's"—loss, loyalty, and lack of control. One 16-year-old stated his loss this way: "I like my dad so much and wanted his attention, and my stepmom came in and took it all away." Another teenager spoke of the loyalty conflicts she had, saying, "I feel caught between my parents because they keep arguing about me." A young adult remembered lack of control when he commented, "My mom was stricter than my dad, and my stepdad took over and was even more strict. It was like a military camp."

ISSUES FOR CHILDREN AT DIFFERENT AGES

The age of the children is an important factor in the type of responses they have to these issues. Following are specific suggestions for three main age groups for ways their families can address them.

Preschool

Toddlers. These young children may become anxious and fearful of separation from their parent. They may regress into bed-wetting and earlier habits and have a strong need for nurturance and care. If they are not caught between hostile parents and stepparents, they accept stepparents more quickly than do older children.

Ages 3–5 Years. These children are similar to the toddlers, but with an important additional response—magical thinking in which they may believe that their negative thoughts have been responsible for the separation of the family. They need appropriate control in their lives and reassurance that their thoughts are not responsible for all the family changes.

Helpful Suggestions

- Assist parenting adults in providing adequate and predictable nurturance and care.

- Encourage the children's two households to cooperate. Visits may be infrequent, but they need to be regular (Isaacs & Leon, 1988).
- Older children can benefit from having a calendar, marked with two colors, to show which days they will be in each of their homes.
- There are helpful books about divorce and remarriage to be read to children in these age groups. (See Resources section.)

Elementary School

Ages 6–12 Years. School-age children tend to become angry and depressed at the time of a divorce, but they may be even more so at the time of the remarriage. They often consider that their unacceptable behavior caused the divorce, and they tend to have many fantasies that they can reunite their divorced parents. At times, they may make conscious attempts to do this by excluding the stepparent or exhibiting other behavior that aims to bring the two original parents together.

This is a developmental period during which children become judgmental and form strong loyalty attachments. They tend to take sides as they view one parent as being "right" and the other as being "wrong." Hostile ex-spouses often encourage this behavior.

Changes in ordinal position in the family are important for these children, i.e., becoming a middle child in the stepfamily instead of the oldest or youngest as they were in their previous family. This can produce profound changes for children that may go unrecognized by the adults.

Helpful Suggestions

- Encourage the adults to change the children's routines gradually and only as much as necessary.
- Keep children informed about plans and general arrangements.

- When children return from their other household, share with them what has taken place during their absence, and refrain from pushing them to share information about their activities while they have been away. Do not comment negatively when they do share information regarding their time in their other household.

Adolescents

Adolescents are dealing with three important developmental issues during these years:

1. Their growing need for individuation from the family
2. Developing their own identity
3. Their emerging sexuality

These developmental tasks can cause stress and emotional tension in any type of family; in themselves, they are not problems created because there is a stepfamily. Unfortunately, many parents and stepparents who are forming new remarriage families with adolescents do not recognize that the teenagers' resistance to family closeness is often related to their developmental stage. If the adults are helped to recall their own teenage years, they are usually more able to let go of unrealistic expectations that their children will welcome their attempts to create "one big happy family."

In stepfamilies, adolescents frequently choose to change their residential arrangements, not necessarily because of difficulties within the household in which they are living most of the time, but rather because of the need to develop their own identity. Adolescents who have lived primarily with one parent following a divorce may wish to change their living arrangements so that they can learn more about their other parent.

A therapeutic task may be to help the adults involved in these changes to understand this adolescent search for identity and to work together with the other household to arrange a residential change, if indicated. Frequently, therapists need to help the adults of one household deal with their sadness as they "let go" of some of their contact with their teenage children. Statistically, this is a time during which there are many residential shifts among adolescents in stepfamilies; a large number of them are arranged between the two households with no formal custody changes by the court (White & Booth, 1985). At times, when adolescents do not feel able to discuss these household changes with their residential parents or step-parents, they can provoke situations that result in their being sent to live with their other parent. Obviously, this is not a positive way to bring about changes in residence. If adolescents cannot discuss this change with their parent and stepparent, they and/or their parents may seek therapy to get help with this issue.

In response to their emerging sexuality, teens may withdraw from stepsiblings of the opposite sex in order to control the sexual feelings that they are just beginning to experience. In response to sexually charged feelings regarding a stepparent, they may reject the attempts of that adult to form a warm relationship.

A comment made in retrospect by a young man who grew up in a stepfamily illustrates these dynamics:

> I was always thinking about girls, and I was always thinking about sex. And one of my fantasy objects was my stepsister. This was particularly tough because I felt both attracted to women and afraid of women, and there she was in various states of undress. Whether she actually was or not I really don't remember. I was attracted to her, and I was curious about her both as an individual and as a symbol. She was too close to ignore. I couldn't distance myself from her in that house.
>
> Another one of my objects was my stepmother. And that was even worse! It was even more threatening to me because I was attracted to her sexually and I went out to her emotionally, too. There was a lot

there in my head. Really my fear about my sexual feelings toward my stepmother kept me from expressing some of my positive emotions towards her. (Visher & Visher, 1979, p. 177)

Helpful Suggestions

- As a rule teenagers do not talk easily about sexual feelings, and therapists may need to normalize the existence of such feelings in stepfamilies by referring to their existence in a matter-of-fact manner. This can allow the young person to retain or gain self-esteem, which may be suffering because they consider their sexual responses to be "sick" or "bad." It needs to be clear, however, that there is a difference between feelings and behavior. Although having such emotions is not unusual, acting on them within the household is not acceptable behavior.
- Alert the adults to the needs of their adolescent children for privacy and for a suitable "dress code" in the household.
- Be sure the adults understand that while the children all benefit from being with adults who are affectionate with each other, passion needs to be reserved for the bedroom.
- Work with the adults to help them understand and allow the adolescents to have contact with their other parent in their search to discover "who I am."
- Help the adults to understand the importance of peers to teenagers and the young people's developmental need to move toward increased independence.

COMMON ISSUES FOR CHILDREN

Observation and clinical experience suggests that the following issues are ones that impact most children, particularly older ones. The first six are marked with an asterisk because they were listed by children 12–19 years old as being their most stressful situations among the 33 items on a questionnaire given to them (Lutz, 1983):

* Hearing your biological parents argue (e.g., over the phone or at the door) and say bad things about each other
* Not being able to see your other parent
* Having your parent and stepparent fight
* Feeling "caught in the middle" between your two birth parents
* Adjusting to new rules set by your stepparent
* Accepting discipline from a stepparent
  Being blamed for everything that goes wrong
  Having your parent do more for stepchildren than for you
  Needing to share your room with other children in your household
  Having the feeling of not being wanted
  Wishing it could all change and go back the way it was before the divorce
  Having a stepparent tell you what to do
  Feeling like it's up to you to make this new family work OK.

In general, children respond to family changes and tensions with anger and depression. While all children experience loss, loyalty conflicts, and lack of control, young children particularly respond to loss, while children of ages 9–13 may be dealing with more severe loyalty conflicts than older or younger children. Adolescents usually are especially angry and depressed because many changes are taking place over which they have little or no control.

In therapy, helping parents and stepparents to understand the concerns of their children and act in ways to be helpful to them is a major avenue of support for children, particularly when they are young and dependent on their family. Conversely, working directly with children can also be helpful, particularly as they mature and become less dependent on their family. When the remarried couple has gained adequate ability to work together on meeting stepfamily challenges, seeing the household together, and including others as indicated, the result is increased communication and understanding between family members. At all times during therapy, whether seeing one individual or the entire family, the importance of thinking in supra family system terms is essential.

EFFECTIVE PARENTING OF CHILDREN IN STEPFAMILIES

There is very little education or preparation for adults in raising children in any type of family. With the added complexity and the unique dynamics of stepfamilies, parents and stepparents benefit greatly from parenting education. Our stepfamily therapy research has revealed that many stepfamily adults seek therapy because of the chaos in their families and concerns involving their children. They need help in discussing ways in which to reduce the chaos.

According to Weston (1993), approximately 80 percent of adults seeking therapy need basic education in how to "parent" the children in their stepfamily, while the rest also need individual therapeutic support to enhance their ability to deal with the children's issues. Weston says that parenting skills can be taught and that the beginning of therapy provides an important window of opportunity to help parents and stepparents learn to better parent their children.

To summarize her approach, adults need to understand a few key points :

- Children feel small and limited in their control.
- Their task is to learn about the world and their place in it.

- Their feelings are their emotional responses to situations.
- They have lots of feelings and things to say.
- Their behavior is their way of communicating because it is only as they mature that they will have the words with which to express themselves.
- They need different things from the adults depending on their developmental level.

As we have discussed earlier, until integration is well underway, stepfamilies usually are chaotic and disorganized. In their efforts to calm the household, the adults often exacerbate the situation because they have little understanding of why the children are behaving in ways that create tension. Building on what Weston outlines, the couple will be able to improve the function of the household if they:

- Look at stepfamily life from the viewpoint of the children, keeping in mind the children's developmental needs at various ages.
- Determine what the children's behavior is saying that they need.
- Find productive ways in which to meet the needs of the children as much as possible.

The following therapy example illustrates these points:

Whenever nine-year-old Terry's stepbrother Hank came for the weekend Terry's behavior disintegrated. In the car he would fight with seven-year-old Hank sitting beside him in the back seat, and tease him unmercifully when they got out of the car. Terry's mother and stepfather were distraught and the weekends degenerated into emotional scenes primarily involving Terry's behavior. When the couple was coached by their therapist to spend time analyzing the situation from Terry's point of view, they soon began to see things from his perspective and understand what his behavior was telling them. They realized that Terry sat in the front seat of the car with them except when Hank was present. Terry was telling them he felt abandoned by them when he was in the back seat. His mother and stepfather let Terry know they understood and gave the boys turns to be in the front while the one in the back seat had a special toy. In a short while Terry no longer responded negatively to being in the back, and then he began to enjoy having Hank there too.

In the house the problem for Terry appeared to be Hank's wanting to play with his toys. Instead of admonishing Terry for not sharing, the adults recognized Terry's need to have the choice of which toys he was willing for Hank to borrow. They purchased a few new toys for each boy and provided Hank with a drawer to keep his toys in when he was not with them. This drawer was "off limits" for Terry, and thus both boys were in control of their own possessions. As the boys slowly approached each other they found they enjoyed making things together with Legos, and both enjoyed running dump trucks and other vehicles in the yard when the weather was nice. Tense weekends slowly became pleasant times for all of them.

Table 6.1 outlines five major issues faced by children in stepfamilies, examples of their common emotional and behavioral responses to these situations, and the needs that the children may be expressing. The final column gives a few suggestions for the adults on how to respond to the children's needs. The table is discussed in the following section in some detail.

SETTLING INTO A STEPFAMILY

When individuals in stepfamilies begin living together, they have no history as a family; for children and adults the household feels unfamiliar and strange. Even if the house is a familiar one for some stepfamily members, there is a strangeness that comes from the presence of new people and their belongings. The children have not chosen these changes and accompanying losses; in addition, they may be moving back and forth between two unfamiliar households with different ways of operating. No wonder that early days in a stepfamily are upsetting to most children. If the adults are able to understand the situation from the children's viewpoint and make an effort to meet their needs, the settling in process can go more smoothly and quickly.

The loss, the loyalty issues, and the extent of their feeling overwhelmed and out of control arises partly because the children's two parents are in two different places. Empirical research and clinical observation indicate that in most instances children wish to remain in contact with both of their parents. Even when a parent has died, children want access to memories of that parent. Until children are late teenagers, they are dependent on their parent and stepparent to provide this access.

While household units need to have boundaries around them to ensure privacy and ensure their area of responsibility and control, the boundaries must be permeable enough for the children to have access to both households.

One way to help the adults to understand is by drawing two circles, overlapping because there are children who are members of both households, with semi-permeable boundaries at the point of their overlap (Exhibit 6.1).

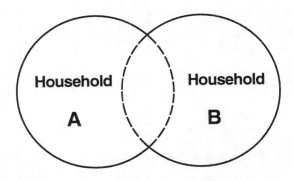

Exhibit 6.1. Overlapping Households.

Table 6.1
CHILDREN IN STEPFAMILIES: SETTLING IN

Stepfamily Situations	Emotional Responses	Behavioral Responses	Needs Being Expressed	Meeting Children's Needs
1. Many losses—family, friends, home, school, parental attention	Sad, depressed, angry	Cry, regress, run away, withdraw, lash out	Access to both parents—emotional and physical	Gates in boundaries around households, one-on-one time with each parent, caring words and actions
2. No control over the changes in their lives	Overwhelmed, small, and totally out of control. As they grow bigger, still out of control in many areas	Attempt to gain control—failing in school, fighting, threatening to live elsewhere, ignoring adults, creating havoc	Control in their lives	Control appropriate for children's maturity—offer choices of food, room arrangement, school activities
3. Many transitions as they move between households	Pushed by adults to adjust immediately to many differences	Cry, slam doors, will not talk	Time to shift households and settle in after transitions	Adult patience and time to adjust, support for "transition rituals"

4. Different roles and rules in their two households	Confused and apprehensive	Disobey, argue, withdraw, have tantrums	Clarity as to roles, rules, and expectations	Communication between adults and children, family meetings, no criticism of differences between households
5. Often caught between hostile parents	Trapped in a no-win situation between parents they love	Make excessive attempts to please parents, refuse to go to Mother's or Father's house, negative behavior, talk against other household, take sides	To get out of the "middle," freedom to love both parents and enjoy both households	Adults leave them out of hostile interchanges, cooperation between all parenting adults regarding children, permission to love both parents and stepparents and enjoy both households

Another way of visualizing the situation for children is in terms of the concept of dual citizenship. As they journey from one place to the other, it can be like an international journey because there are differences in food, language, money, religion, climate, space, and customs. It takes time to prepare oneself for such a trip and often there is tension before leaving, and also after arriving. No wonder children become anxious and need time to adjust and feel more comfortable. Taking familiar objects with them can help. As the two countries become familiar and predictable, having dual citizenship can be rich and rewarding *unless the two countries are at war*. This hostile situation leads to loss, divided loyalties, apprehension, and fear. Unfortunately, many children find themselves in precisely that situation ranging from a cold war standoff to bitter and destructive fighting between their two households.

Frances and Bobbie are two children caught in such a battle: Frances, ten, and Bobbie, seven, lived most of the time with their mother, and saw their father, David, and stepmother, Rosemary, occasionally. Their mother, Estelle, had not remarried and she had remained bitter and resentful towards her former husband even though she was the one who had wanted the divorce. Estelle had not accepted Daniel's marriage to Rosemary, and she was constantly saying negative things to Frances and Bobbie about their father and stepmother. Not surprisingly, the children sometimes cried when they left their mother and they remained sullen and silent or became belligerent during the weekend when they were with Daniel and Rosemary.

Rosemary felt the rejection of the children and kept trying to please them. It seemed to her that the harder she tried, the more belligerent they became. Rosemary grew increasingly upset and finally made an appointment with a family therapist because she felt she must be doing something wrong. The therapist saw Rosemary and listened to her story of the situation. The therapist suggested that the children might be reacting to feeling caught between their two households rather than to any behavior of hers. This reassured Rosemary and she felt somewhat better.

The therapist saw the couple together for several months and helped the two of them to strengthen their relationship. Their bond had suffered because of the lack of support Daniel was giving to his wife. He feared a greater loss of relationship with his children and he said nothing when they were disrespectful both to him and to Rosemary. In addition, Daniel spent the time his children were with them giving them all his attention and excluding Rosemary. He also criticized his wife for withdrawing from the children and said it was no wonder the children were tense and argumentative.

In the therapy sessions, Daniel agreed with Rosemary's impression of what the children were being told about both of them by their mother; a good friend of his had told him about hearing Estelle talk negatively to the children. Daniel became willing to consider the children's behavior as being their way of responding to the hostility between the two households rather than their response to Rosemary.

Daniel and Rosemary had also made negative remarks about Estelle. Now they recognized that the children overheard some of their criticisms of Estelle's behavior and were upset by this. They also understood that they had antagonized Estelle. Because they cared about the children, Daniel and Rosemary began to control this behavior. They also told Frances and Bobbie that they realized it might be hard for them to leave their mom and come to be with them for a weekend. The children nodded, but did not respond verbally. However, the situation improved when the children did not experience Rosemary and their father as being critical of their mother even though their mother continued to be sarcastic and noncooperative on the telephone when making arrangements with Daniel.

Two events made a significant change in these households. In a telephone conversation with Estelle, at the suggestion of the therapist to be a little supportive, Daniel spoke about the good care she was giving the children. Daniel experienced a positive change in their conversations after that. Shortly thereafter, an 11-year-old son of a good friend of Estelle's killed himself, leaving a note saying he missed his father, whom he did not see. Estelle was shocked and asked Daniel if he would like to see the children more often. This pleased Daniel very much. Reluctantly, Estelle came to accept that Rosemary also had a place in the children's lives. Slowly, the barriers between the two households came down and the children's access became free in both directions. When the children were no longer dealing with severe loyalty conflicts, they began to enjoy both of their households, and their happiness helped create more satisfaction for all the adults.

Another example of a successful therapeutic intervention occurred with another family in which two teens were shifting households every other weekend, and these formerly satisfactory arrangements began to fall apart.

Two teenage sisters, Suzie and Lena, spent equal time in their two households. Suddenly they began to rebel at the changes and said they wanted to live with their mother and stepfather and have shorter visits with their father and stepmother. Fortunately, the adults in both households had always made a point of giving the girls as many choices as they could—what activities they would like, whether or not they would like to have friends come to visit, how to fix their rooms in each of their houses. With this background, it was relatively easy for the adults to understand that something was changing for the girls and they all came together with a counselor to discuss the situation.

In two sessions, the communication made it clear what was happening. Suzie was now 16 and Lena was 14. Their two households were not in the same school district, but the two couples had been able to see that the girls were taken to school and picked up each day. Now, however, their peers were becoming very important to them and several of the girls' friends were complaining that they never knew where to call them on the telephone. The girls had been happy with the control they had been given and the choices they had made, but now they were feeling a lack of control. With the assistance of the counselor, the adults and young people together were able to work out satisfactory new residential arrangements.

THERAPY WITH CHILDREN

Children can be very clear in expressing the three feelings we spoke about at the beginning of this chapter, namely: loss, loyalty, and lack of control:

"It's not easy having two moms, because you keep missing someone and I want to be with everyone," sighed an eight-year-old girl. A boy, age 13, with a father, stepfather, grandfathers, and stepgrandfathers, was planning his bar mitzvah and was worried about whom he should invite to be part of the service. "I'd feel guilty if everybody wasn't part of it. I'm going to invite everybody, and if one won't come, that's too bad."

And a 16-year-old girl said, "She (stepmother) felt she gained a power over me the day she married my father. Before that she'd been my friend. It needs to be gradual. Just because she said, 'I do,' she changed things right away."

Here are some specific suggestions for helping children when they are being seen directly:

1. Provide Emotional Support.

Children's emotions are routinely intense and mixed. Many therapists find that anger and grief are always present in the stepchildren they see. Children are helped when therapists acknowledge the existence of initial difficulties, letting children know that stepfamilies can become families that are full of respect and joy. Children need to feel that society's generally negative assessment of their type of family need not be a permanent handicap to integration.

2. Validate Feelings.

Unfortunately, children's feelings may not be accepted or validated by their parents and stepparents. The adults are often invested in having a "happy family" from the first day, and as a result they are not able to tolerate negative emotions from their children. When you look at early stepfamily life from the point of view of children, it is easy to understand many of their reactions to all the changes. Therapy provides children with an opportunity to express their feelings without being criticized. Understanding the cause, and accepting the validity of their feelings can certainly be of major importance for children, even as they need to know that their family is a valued family.

3. Help with Mourning of Losses.

Change of any kind brings loss and this is a predominant feature of stepfamilies since death or divorce precedes the formation of stepfamilies. Children often have not been permitted to express their sorrow about their earlier losses, and now they experience loss of time and attention from a parent, as well as other more obvious losses that have been added to the original ones. As a rule, only after children have been able to acknowledge their grief and give expression to it can they begin to acknowledge some gains in their new situation.

4. Help Children Feel Less Helpless.

As we have stressed earlier, feeling in control is of basic importance to people of any age. In fact, children often would rather consider that they are responsible for the breakup of their original family than feel that they were helpless to prevent what happened. Before one attempts to remove their guilt or their sense of responsibility, it is advisable to first help them gain autonomy over aspects of their lives appropriate for their ages. If they relinquish their sense of responsibility for what has taken place prior to gaining positive mastery over other aspects of their present lives, they can become depressed because they feel totally helpless. The more freedom of choice, appropriate for their age, that children can have, the more they will experience control and mastery over their lives. A perception of lack of control may be one factor contributing to a child's anger and depression. Increased autonomy may alleviate these feelings and reduce rebellious and unacceptable behavior. Older children may be able to talk with their parents and stepparents to work out more areas of autonomy in their lives; younger children frequently need their therapists to help the adults give them more control over their lives. This was true for 10-year-old Craig:

> Craig, at nine, was an athletic child who loved playing soccer and skateboarding with his friends. When his parents divorced, he continued to live with his mother and sister in the same neighborhood. However, when his mother remarried the next year, the new couple purchased a house in a different school district. Craig no longer attended a school with a devoted soccer coach, and no longer saw his friends after school. He was not a shy child, but he had entered school in the middle of the school year after the children had already formed peer friendship groups. Craig's schoolwork plummeted and he became disruptive on the playground and at home.

On the recommendation of school personnel, Craig's mother took him to see a child psychologist. After talking with Craig, the psychologist made an appointment with his mother and stepfather. During the appointment, the psychologist outlined the many losses for Craig that had resulted from the move and suggested that there might be areas in which the adults could help Craig regain important supports and areas of control.

Craig joined his mother and stepfather for the next appointment. Together, they talked about times Craig could ask former friends over for visits. Craig also wanted to ask two boys from his new school class to go to a circus that was coming to town. This worked out, and he began to do other things with his new friends. He also chose to join the school hockey team, and when the team traveled to play against other schools his mother and stepfather went along as enthusiastic supporters. Craig's good nature reappeared and his school work improved dramatically. He soon had a number of activities to choose from every day after school.

In three different families we know about, the feelings of the teens changed dramatically when they were permitted to use a family automobile. Not only did it signify trust in them and their judgment, it also allowed them an important control they had not had previously in their lives. In two situations, it was the stepparent's car they borrowed. As would be expected, the adolescents were particular impressed by the fact that it was their stepparent who was trusting them. Younger children may be given the freedom to choose their clothes, hair style, or what school activities they wish to join.

Choices bring freedom from the control of others, and the happiness of children in any family can increase with the power that comes from having the opportunity to make choices in areas commensurate with their maturity.

5. Reassure Children Whose Parent Has Disappeared.

In a few situations, children do not wish to have further contact with their other parent. However, the majority of children prefer to have contact with both of their parents following a divorce in the family. If the other parent disappears, children frequently feel that the parent didn't love them; otherwise, he or she would not have abandoned them. The children often believe that there is something wrong with them or that they are unlovable, and their self-esteem drops.

In these situations, the task in therapy becomes one of restoring children's self-confidence, as well as helping them to deal with the sadness about their loss. One way of raising their self-esteem is by helping them understand that the disappearance of their parent is due to something that is inside that parent, an "adult problem." This can be very reassuring. Some children will want to know what precipitated their parent's withdrawal. This is not a question that ordinarily can be answered, or whose answer would necessarily be helpful. However, children often form their own opinions about their parent's motives. Helping them find an explanation that does not include them can often allow children to relax and relinquish the feelings that they were responsible for their parent's disappearance.

6. Release Children from Responsibility for Parents.

During the single-parent household phase, children often become the caretakers of the adults. When discussing memories of what it had been like for him at the time of his parents' divorce, a teenager said, "I saw your problems as worse than mine, and I didn't want to burden you with my feelings."

Even after a remarriage, children may continue to take responsibility for their parents. For example, they may decide to stay with a single parent whom they feel "needs" them, rather than to live with their other parent who has remarried. This may occur even when the adults have worked out a plan for change of residence for the teenager in what they believe to be the best interest of their child. In another type of situation, even young children submerge their own needs because they are attempting to meet all of the needs of the parent.

When there is hostility between the parents, the children are especially vulnerable. Several adolescents illustrated this when they talked of not letting their mothers know when they were ill and might need to see a doctor, because their mother would then get into an argument with her former husband over who would pay the doctor's bill. Children may need help to understand that an adult's behavior is the adult's responsibility.

7. Accept and Clarify Anger.

There can be a great deal of anger floating around in a stepfamily, and often it is displaced from its actual target. Children fear losing their parents' affection. Therefore, if the children become angry, it is less threatening for them to be angry at their stepparents, whom they are less afraid of losing. Stepparents often are the target of anger that the stepchildren actually feel toward one or both of their parents.

In therapy with children, it can be important for them to have their anger accepted (with no family adult being there to have hurt feelings or attempting to deflect the anger in some way). It can also be important for the children to clarify the source of their anger so that situations can be resolved, or at least understood. Ten-year-old Janie illustrates this:

> *Janie:* I hate my stepmother. She's mean, and I wish she'd go away.
> *Therapist:* What does she do that you don't like?
> *Janie:* She treats her son like a baby. He's a little older than I am. I wouldn't want her to treat me that way.
> *Therapist:* How does she treat him like a baby?

Janie: She keeps getting him things he likes to eat, and the other day he was sick and had to stay in bed. We had to go up and have lunch with him in his room. (*With tears streaming down her cheeks*) My mother wouldn't do that. It's such a baby thing to do. My mother would let me look after myself.

Therapist: Perhaps there are times you'd like a little attention like that. Most kids do. I guess that's particularly true when they're not feeling well.

Janie: No, I wouldn't. NO! My mom doesn't spoil me!

Therapist: Oh, you think it's spoiling your stepbrother. What do you mean by that?

Janie: He'll want us to eat with him all the time, even when he's not sick.

Therapist: Is that what happens?

Janie: No, but it might.

Therapist: If you were sick at her house do you think your stepmom would do the same thing for you?

Janie: I suppose so.

Therapist: Um hum...maybe you wish a little bit that your mom might do that just a little bit.

Janie: Maybe, a little.

Therapist: Things like that usually make children angry. Maybe you are a little angry at your mom sometimes.

Janie: Maybe.

Therapist: So it's hard having your stepmom be that way when someone's not feeling well?

Janie: (*In tears*) I don't want my stepmom to be a good mom. I want my mom to be a good mom.

Therapist: So I guess you're really upset sometimes with your mom, but it's easier to be mad at your stepmom than at her. I'll bet they each do a

lot of things that are different—some things you
like a lot, and some you wish were different, and
it makes you angry.

8. Help Children "Out of the Middle."

Children frequently get caught in the middle between their
two households when there is tension or hostility between
the adults in those households. At times, the children are
used as messengers and spies, and at other times they are
caught in the hostility. Children express this in many
ways, such as: "They're shooting arrows at each other and
the arrows go right through me," or, "They're throwing a
ball back and forth between them, and I'm the ball." With
encouragement from a therapist, many adolescent children can say to one or both parents, "I don't want to carry
messages back and forth. Telephone or write. You two talk
to each other, please." Often, the adults have not been
aware of the difficult position their children are caught in,
and such a request from the young person states the
problem clearly and can make a difference.

Younger children may not be able to be direct. With the
child's permission, a therapist may need to talk to the
adults. Hopefully, they will then become aware of their
behavior and its detrimental effect on the children. Adults
can be motivated for change by their love for their children, and for many this is strong enough to allow them to
leave the children out of the middle. In one instance, a
sensitive mother had not recognized that it was upsetting
to her young son whenever she spoke angrily to her former
husband, the boy's father, whom he loved. When the boy's
therapist made her aware of her son's upset around this
behavior, the mother quickly changed. Although she did
not suddenly lose her anger at her former husband, she
made certain that she did not discuss emotionally upsetting topics with the boy's father if her son was present or
could hear. This solution worked satisfactorily in this
household.

9. Help Children Talk About Rather Than Act Out Their Feelings.

As was discussed earlier in this chapter, young children have little ability to put their feelings into words. Instead, they behave in ways that frequently upset the adults. As a result, the children become more upset because the adults do not understand the message in the behavior. Even older children can be caught in the same type of cycle, although they have more verbal ability because of their growing maturity.

Part of the problem for children is the fact that they often express their emotions verbally, but the adults do not listen or become angry at what they are saying. First of all, therapists may need to take time to build trust so that the children become willing to talk about how they feel. Then the therapist may be able to help by having the children write a letter to their parents or communicate with them in some less threatening way. Perhaps they can all meet together with the therapist.

Many divorced biological parents come together only around negative interactions, as when their son or daughter gets into trouble at school, or when a child is ill and needs medical attention. For some children, there is a secondary gain in creating negative happenings to bring their parents together. We have often heard young adults say that when they saw their biological parents being together in a crisis they felt a surge of hope that they would get back together permanently, only to be terribly disappointed when it didn't happen. Parents cannot react only to crisis situations; they also need to connect with one another when there is some positive reason to get together. Including stepparents as well makes it harder for the children to fantasize that cooperation between their parents sends a signal of a parental reconciliation.

In all such situations, the task is to normalize and accept the children's feelings, put them into words, and help the adults to understand what is taking place. Former spouses need to come together in connection with both positive and negative events, and children need to be able to talk to the adults about their wishes to get to know or be with their other parent. Often, they do need the therapist's support in communication.

10. Parental Reorganization of Time Is Not Loss of Love.

One of the most upsetting things for children following the remarriage of a parent is the loss of time and attention from that parent. That adult now has a new partner, and perhaps other children, to respond to. Often, the adults consider that they need to do everything together as a family to hurry the process of "becoming one big happy family." It goes unnoticed that the reorganization of time is a loss for the children. Therapists can help children to see that less time does not mean less love. Children may be able to understand it by using the example of their reactions to their toys or to their friends. Many situations can change; the time each child may spend with certain toys or friends may change, but their caring for them is not changed.

This is an area in which therapists may need to educate the adults to the need for one-on-one times in their household. In one new stepfamily, it turned out that the husband and the wife's two children were all feeling that they did not have enough of her attention. She, in turn, felt pulled apart trying to give them all what they wanted. The therapist saw the four of them together and demonstrated how important one-on-one time is to individuals. The therapist also demonstrated the need to take turns. With excitement the woman said, "Oh, that means that I can do things with each of my children, and that my husband and I can go to the movies by ourselves sometimes!" The boy and his stepfather began to plan to go fishing together, and he and his stepdaughter said they wanted to think about what they would do with each other. There was less mother–child time than in their single-parent household, but not less love. They were going to plan special time with undivided parental attention and also some stepparent–stepchild.

11. Use Adjuncts to Therapy.

There are many good books for children of all ages that deal with divorce and remarriage. Some may be available from local libraries or bookstores, and many are available from the Stepfamily Association of America. There is a list of books for children in the Resources section of this book.

Children's groups dealing with divorce and remarriage also are helpful. (See Resources.) Schools and churches as well as mental health agencies are beginning to provide such groups. They can act to normalize stepfamily and divorce situations for children and give them the experience of knowing they are not alone or to blame for the family changes they are experiencing.

SUMMARY

Children are often amazingly resilient and adaptable to changes, provided that the rules in each setting are clear and unambiguous. While their way of expressing feelings with behavior can sometimes make things difficult and result in the child being brought in to the therapist as the "identified patient," fairly simple interventions along the lines discussed in this section can often make a big difference. In many cases, younger children do not need to be seen if the adults can achieve more understanding of what is causing the reactions. Therefore, an important intervention can be simply to work with the parents in an effort to help them to understand what is happening in the family and what can be done to make things go better. At other times, it can be valuable to see the household or households together to help the children and adults learn to communicate better with each other attention.

7

SUCCESSFUL
STEPFAMILIES

Until now, this book has dealt with information and ideas that are the result of stepfamily research and the clinical experience and observations of mental health professionals we have had the opportunity to talk with during our stepfamily therapy workshop. We would like to summarize the material and conclude with some comments and ideas that have come from stepfamilies who have successfully threaded their way through the maze of challenges that can occur in any stepfamily.

Not only do the families cited here exemplify healthy remarriage families, they illustrate what it takes to create and maintain warm and rewarding relationships in any type of family. Indeed, with the consciousness that accompanies almost all emotions and actions during their integration process, the experiences of stepfamily members can teach lessons to all families. Interactions that can be crucial to the formation of successful stepfamily relationships can facilitate and enhance the functioning of all families. Remarried parents, stepparents, and children living in remarriage families teach us important lessons about embracing diversity, dealing with the inevitable losses in life, and not taking our important relationships for granted.

Stepfamily members are becoming more comfortable about telling their stories, and we keep learning from those with whom we have contact. It is exciting and illuminating, and is an important validation of the research and clinical impressions we have discussed. The following information comes from these contacts and also from a recent book by Kelley (1995), which is a report of the detailed study of 20 successful stepfamilies who discuss their views about the ingredients that go into creating a successful remarriage.

Overwhelmingly, these families support the importance of having realistic expectations of stepfamily life, forming a strong and unified couple relationship, creating important rituals and traditional ways of doing things, developing positive steprelationships, and cooperating with the children's other household. Following are many ideas and suggestions in these important areas, and also the things in their families that stepfamily members have appreciated.

INGREDIENTS OF SUCCESSFUL STEPFAMILIES

Have Realistic Expectations

It is important to have realistic expectations; this quote from one family echoes the words of many families:

> "We tried to make our family a picture postcard family, where everyone is tightly knit into one unit...it didn't work, and we got frustrated and it made things worse." (Kelley, 1995, p. 81)

The major topics stepfamilies outline are:

- Instant love is a myth. It is necessary for stepparents to come in slowly. Don't come in "like the cheerleader of the Western World."
- Do not attempt to force relationships. Be patient and let them develop at their own speed.
- Parents need to discipline their own children, except when the children are very young. The

adults cannot expect the stepparent to take this role until a relationship has formed.

Strengthen Couple Relationships

It is the couple relationship that holds the family together and allows the other relationships to develop and the functioning of the family to settle down. This is the basic theme of virtually all the families who feel they have "made it." They maintain that it is a good couple relationship that sets the foundation for everything else and acts as the main element that pulls the family through the hard spots. Specific suggestions for doing this are:

- There is a need for couple privacy and space, as well as for individual space for adults.
- The couple needs to work out financial rules in a manner suitable for the situation of the family. This is an area of considerable concern raised by the families studied by Kelley (1995). Having a clear and definite system of money management contributed to the successful functioning of the family.
- All stepfamily members have to learn to put up with things they are not used to and do not like.
- The adults need alone time, and the couple needs special times away from the children.
- Both adults need to share family responsibilities.
- Having strong social support networks is important.

The following quotes express the importance of the couple relationship:

"My husband has truly committed himself to our current family and supports me when I get frustrated."

"My relationship with my wife comes first and we stand together in dealing with the family."

Establish Constructive Rituals

"Family rituals are regulatory patterns that help consolidate family identity and provide structure and cohesiveness" (Hartman & Laird, 1983, p. 320). They are especially important for stepfamilies as they help the individuals to feel connected and part of the new unit. They also give a predictability to day-to-day activities that can provide the family members with more sense of control over their lives:

- Day-to-day rituals are important. Bedtime stories, household chores, choice of meals, alone time with parent and with stepparent are all "together times" that need to be planned and regular, but not necessarily lengthy.
- Flexibility is important here because you have the needs of many people to take into consideration. As a result, new rituals may need to be designed: celebrating both Hanukkah and Christmas; alternating Thanksgivings with the other household; celebrating on a day other than the traditional date.
- At children's special times (graduations, weddings), put aside adult animosities for this limited time so that the children can enjoy having both of their parents and their stepparents participate.
- Family meetings can be good times to deal with difficult issues in a positive way. Give family members turns in running the meeting. All ideas count equally. (The adults retain veto power for truly unworkable suggestions.)
- Be creative in working out the roles and rules for the household. These issues are excellent ones for discussion in family meetings.

Build Satisfactory Step-Relationships

This is an area in which children in stepfamilies, as well as the adults, have given many suggestions because this is an

area of considerable importance to them. In these successful families, the comments of the children indicate a
thoughtfulness and empathy for the adults, as well as a
sensitivity for their own situation, when, for example, they
say, "The adults in stepfamilies try very hard to make
things work out," and "It's hard for everyone, not just us."
Other suggestions include:

- Stepparents come in slowly and do not start disciplining immediately.
- Stepparents need to be sure not to compete with the
  parent in the other household.
- Find special areas to share with stepchildren, for
  example, if you like fishing and your stepchild is
  interested, use this activity to build a relationship.
  However, the activity should not be competitive
  with the children's relationships to a parent who is
  elsewhere.
- Children and adults need to be respectful to each
  other.
- Stepparents need to support one-on-one time between the parent and each child, and also arrange
  one-on-one times with stepchildren to build those
  important relationships.
- Respect and liking are more important than love.
- Ask the children what they want to call their
  stepparent. This topic may take some negotiation.
- Building trust is important. As mentioned earlier,
  several young adults talked about their stepfather's allowing them to drive their car, and one
  put the dramatic shifts in the relationship this way:
  "I felt trusted. It really made a difference in our
  relationship."
- Parents should make room for the stepparent to be
  part of the family. One family sent the young child
  to her stepfather to have her shoes tied, rather than
  having the mother always be the person to do it. In
  another family in which each adult had children, at
  allowance time the stepparent was the one who

gave the allowances to his or her stepchildren.

- Do not give away household items from the past without first asking older children if they want them.
- Good communication and a sense of humor really help.

Deal with the Other Household

The final area to be addressed was the difficult task of working with the children's other household. Children talked of appreciating any show of cooperation, and the adults spoke of the need to respect the children's relationship with their other household. Many stressed the importance and value of working together between households:

"At first I moved twice a week, and that was too confusing. Then I moved every two weeks, but that was too long because whichever family I was with, I began to miss the other family. Every week is just right, and once we found the pattern to work, we just kept it."

"Even though my ex-husband seldom pays child support, the children need to see their father. I would not prevent them from being together even if he never paid his child support. He is a good father to them."

"The first year was difficult. However, we all worked at cooperating. As I have learned to 'share' my children, I can accept their stepmother as a very special person in my children's lives without losing sight of my importance to them. For me, she has become an ally in the job of raising three energetic boys. Everything isn't perfect by any means, but watching them grow up learning that people are to love and that there can't be too many loving people in their lives rises above any momentary envy in me." (Anonymous quote in the newsletter of the Santa Barbara Chapter of Stepfamily Association of America)

Appreciate Stepfamily Rewards

As a rule, adults and children spoke about it taking work and patience, as well as considerable time, to arrive at a rewarding stage in the integration process of their family. As well as talking in general terms about their appreciation of their family life, stepfamily members spoke of particularly rewarding situations and feelings. To quote a few of these:

"When my stepdaughter got married she said to me, 'If it hadn't been for you, I would never have known what a mother is or how to be one.' That statement makes all the difficulties and earlier problems worth it for me." (From a stepmother married to a widower)

"I used to be a pretty rigid guy. I've learned to be much more flexible, and this helps me at work as well as at home." (From a stepfather)

"You learn that you can survive whatever happens to you, and this gives you self-confidence." (From an adult)

"I have a nine-year-old stepson who is acting the way I wish I could have when I was growing up. I had to be old before my time and he fools around and sometimes is a little rebellious. It is fun for me to watch him." (From a stepfather)

And from the children:

"We're even closer than some biological families because we've been through so much together."

"It was really good for me having two families because I had a lot of love."

"Everybody goes through trauma and everybody survives. At the beginning I thought I wouldn't get through. Now I think I'm stronger for it."

"Now there are a lot of new people in my life—and a lot of grandparents. It can be really good, really fun."

"You have more friends, more presents, more celebrations, more adults to love you, and more children in the house to play with or do things with."

We have heard numerous heartwarming and poignant stories from many remarriage families. It appears that stepfamily members nearly always remain consciously aware of their personal interactions. Rewarding interchanges are savored for a long time and remain as a special memory forever because they mark the growth of relationships that were not given by birth. Instead, they were painfully and wondrously created.

CONCLUSION

We have been impressed by the dedication, time, and effort that parents and stepparents devote to creating families that develop into centers of emotional warmth and personal satisfaction. Many remarriage families accomplish this integration process without therapeutic assistance, while others have sought various kinds of support along the way. It is not surprising that help is needed, given the complexity of the process of moving from strangers living together under one roof to a home in which members have a feeling of belonging to a rewarding family unit.

Things are changing gradually. There are more books, more classes and courses, more support and therapy groups, and more awareness of remarriage and ways to make it successful. When there are more societal changes and acceptance, and when even more information, education, and therapeutic knowledge and support are available, it seems not too optimistic to believe that the number of successful remarriage families will steadily increase. This is certainly a goal worth pursuing.

RESOURCES

ADJUNCTS FOR THERAPY, COMMUNITY
RESOURCES AND SUPPORT GROUPS

Stepfamily Association of America

This organization is a good resource for stepfamilies. The Association publishes an excellent small book called *Stepfamilies Stepping Ahead* that explains in simple language what people in new stepfamilies need to know. Many qualified family therapists have found it to be exceedingly useful in helping adults in new stepfamilies. The Association also provides guidance to local chapters throughout the country to assist them in organizing and operating support groups and educational services for stepfamilies. It also publishes a quarterly newsletter, sponsors regional conferences, and offers probably the widest selection of self-help books in the country on divorce and remarriage for stepfamily members and professionals. The Association headquarters is at 215 Centennial Mall S., Lincoln, NE 68508. Phone 1–800–735–0329.

SCHOOL-BASED PROGRAMS

Banana Splits

Contact: Interact Publishing Company
                1825 Gillespie Way, Suite 101
                El Cajon, CA 92020
                Phone: 619–448–1474

A school-based progam for survivors of the divorce wars. It provides manuals for teachers on establishing support groups for elementary, middle school, and high school children. The groups are a helpful adjunct to counseling.

Shapes of Families Today

Contact: Stepfamily Association of America
                215 Centennial Mall S., #212
                Lincoln, NE 68508
                Phone: 1–800–735–0329

The Aring Institute

Contact: Beech Acres
                6681 Beechmont Ave.
                Cincinnati, OH 45230
                Phone: 513–231–6630

This group has extensive experience in the schools and also with children's and parent's educational and support groups outside of school hours.

Rainbows for All Children

Contact: Susie Yehl Marta
                1111 Tower Rd.
                Schaumberg, IL 60173–4305
                Phone: 708–310–1880

This program provides teacher guides and training for regular meetings for children of divorce and remarriage in the schools.

BOOKS

There are many books written for professionals, and for children of all ages and for adults in stepfamilies. Many are not generally available in bookstores or libraries, but they can be ordered from the publisher or from the Stepfamliy Association. Here is a sampling of some of them.

References for Therapists and Counselors

1. Papernow, P. *Becoming a Stepfamily: Patterns of Development in Remarried Families.* San Francisco: Jossey-Bass, 1993. Also suitable for adults in stepfamilies.

Excellent resource on normal development patterns in stepfamilies.

2. Sager, C.J., et al. *Treating the Remarried Family.* New York: Brunner/Mazel, 1983.

This is one of the pioneering books on treament of stepfamilies from a psychoanalytical perspective.

3. Visher,E., & Visher, J. *Stepfamilies: A Guide to Working with Stepparents and Stepchildren.* New York, Brunner/Mazel, 1979. (Also available in paperback under a different title, *Stepfamilies: Myths and Realities.*) Suitable for adults in stepfamilies.

The pioneering book on stepfamily realities.

4. Visher, E., & Visher, J: *Old Loyalties, New Ties: Therapeutic Strategies with Stepfamilies.* New York: Brunner/Mazel, 1988.

The result of 10 years of experience in treament of and teaching about stepfamilies. For therapists and counsellors who wish more detailed information about helping stepfamilies.

5. Browning, S. Treating stepfamilies: Alternatives to traditional family therapy. In K. Pasley & M. Ihinger-Tallman (Eds.), *Stepparenting: Issues in Theory, Research, and Practice.* Westport, CT: Praeger, 1994, pp. 175–198.

A recent contribution to the theory and practice of stepfamily therapy.

References for Adults in Stepfamilies

1. Burns, C. *Stepmotherhood: How to Survive Without Feeeling Frustrated, Left Out, or Wicked.* New York: Times Books, 1986.

A book much appreciated by stepmothers.

2. Burt, M. *Stepfamilies Stepping Ahead.* Lincoln, NE: Stepfamily Association, 1989. (Mentioned under Stepfamily Association of America.)

3. Bernstein, A. *Yours, Mine, and Ours: How Families Change When Remarried Parents Have a Child Together.* New York: W. W. Norton, 1990

The authoritative book about stepfamilies with "our" children.

4. Visher, E., & Visher, J. *How to Win as a Stepfamily* (Second Edition). New York: Brunner/Mazel, 1991.

A help for adults either contemplating remarriage or in new stepfamilies.

5. Twilley, D. *Questions From Dad: A Very Cool Way to Communicate with Kids.* Boston: Tuttle, 1994.

A great help for Dads who want to get in touch with their offspring.

For more suggestions contact Stepfamily Association of America at 1–800–325–0329 for their Educational Resources Catalogue.

References for Children in Stepfamilies

1. Berman, C. *Making It as a Stepfamily.* New York: Harper & Row, 1986.

Easy to read, with suggestions for coping with stepfamily difficulties.

2. Brown, L.K., & Brown, M. *Dinosaurs Divorce.* Boston: Little, Brown, 1986.

Excellent and humorous book providing information for young children about divorce.

3. Getzoff, A., & McClenahan, C. *Stepkids: A Survival Guide for Teenagers in Stepfamilies.* New York: Walker, 1984.

A leading resource for teenagers, and helpful for their adults also.

4. Magid, K., & Schreibmann, W. *Kids Stepfamily Kit* (book and audio tape). Lakewood, CO: KM Productions, 1992.

A cartoon and educational coloring book for young children to help with their reactions to divorce.

5. Lewis, H.C. *All About Families—The Second Time Around.* Atlanta, GA: Peach Tree Publishers, 1980.

Child-oriented information about remarriage.

For more suggestions, contact Stepfamily Association of America at 1–800–735–0329 for their Educational Resources Catalogue.

REFERENCES

Aydintug, C. D. (1995). Former spouse interaction: Normative guidelines and actual behavior. *Journal of Divorce and Remarriage, 22* (3/4), 147–161.

Bender, W. N., & Brandon, L. (1994). Victimization of non-custodial parents, grandparents, and children as a function of sole custody: Views of the advocacy groups and research support. *Journal of Divorce and Remarriage, 21* (3/4), 81–114.

Bohannan, P.C. (1993). Personal communication.

Boss, P., & Greenberg, J. (1984). Family boundary ambiguity: A new variable in family stress theory. *Family Process, 23*, 535–546.

Bray, J. H. (1988). Children's development in early remarriage. In E.M. Hetherington & J. Arasteh (Eds.), *The impact of divorce, single-parenting, and step-parenting on children.* (pp. 279–298). Hillsdale, NJ: Lawrence Erlbaum and Associates.

Bray, J. H. (1992). Family relationships and children's adjustment in clinical and non-clinical stepfather families. *Journal of Family Psychology, 6,* 60–68.

Carter, B., & McGoldrick, M. (1988). *The changing family life cycle: A framework for family therapy* (2nd ed.). New York: Gardner Press.

Chollak, H. (1989). *Stepfamily adaptability and cohesion: A normative study.* Ann Arbor, MI: University Microfilms.

Coale, H. (1993). Personal communication.

Coleman, M., & Ganong, L. (1987). The cultural stereotyping of stepfamilies. In K. Pasley & M. Ihinger–Tallman (Eds.), *Remarriage and stepparenting: Current research and theory* (pp. 19–41). New York: Guilford Press.

Crosbie-Burnett, M. (1984). The centrality of the step relationship: A challenge to family theory and practice. *Family Relations, 33,* 459–463.

Fine, M. A. (1992a). Recent changes in laws affecting stepfamilies: Suggestions for legal reform. *Family Relations, 41,* 334–340.

Fine, M. A. (1992b). Families in the United States: Their current status and future prospects. *Family Relations, 41,* 430–435.

Finkelhor, D. (1994). Current information on the scope and nature of child sexual abuse. *The Future of Children, 42,* 31–53.

Gamache, S. (1993). Personal communication.

Giles-Sims, J. (1995). *A review of current knowledge about child abuse in stepfamilies.* Paper presented at the Fourth International Family Violence Research Conference, Durham, NH.

Glick, P. C. (1989). Remarried families, stepfamilies, and children: A brief demographic profile. *Family Relations, 38,* 24–27.

Glick, P. C. (1991). Address to Annual Conference, Stepfamily Association of America, Lincoln, NE.

Hartman, A., & Laird, J. (1983). *Family-centered social work practice.* New York: Free Press.

Hetherington, E. M. (1989). Coping with family transitions: Winners, losers, and survivors. *Child Development, 60*(1), 1–14.

Hetherington, E. M., Stanley-Hagan, M., & Anderson, E. R. (1989). Marital transitions: A child's perspective. *American Psychologist, 44*(2), 303–312.

Isaacs, M. B., & Leon, G. H. (1988). Remarriage and its

alternatives following divorce: Mother and child adjustment. *Journal of Marital and Family Therapy, 14*(2), 163–173.

Kelley, P. (1995). *Developing healthy stepfamilies: 20 families tell their stories.* Binghamton, NY: Haworth Press.

Kimball, G. (1988). *50–50 parenting: Shared family rewards and responsibilities.* Lexington, MA: Lexington Books.

Kurdek, L. A., & Fine, M. A. (1993). The relation between family structure and young adolescents' appraisal of family climate and parenting behavior. *Journal of Family Issues, 14*, 279–290.

Landau-Stanton, J. (1985). Adolescents, families, and cultural transition: A treatment model. In M. P. Mirkin & S. Koman (Eds.), *Handbook of adolescent and family therapy* (pp. 363–381). New York: Gardner Press.

Landau-Stanton, J. K., Griffiths, J. G., & Mason, G. (1982). The extended family in transition: Clinical implications. In F. Kaslow (Ed.), *The International Book of Family Therapy* (pp. 360–368). New York: Brunner/Mazel.

Lutz, P. (1983). The stepfamily: An adolescent perspective. *Family Relations, 32*, 367–375.

McGoldrick, M., & Carter, B. (1988). Forming a remarried family. In B. Carter & M. McGoldrick (Eds.), *The changing family life cycle: A framework for family therapy* (2nd. ed.). (pp. 399–429). New York: Gardner Press.

McGoldrick, M., & Gerson, R. (1985). *Genograms in family assessment.* New York: W.W. Norton.

Mills, D. M. (1984). A model for stepfamily development. *Family Relations, 33*, 365–372.

Papernow, P. (1991). Personal communication.

Papernow, P. (1993). *Becoming a stepfamily: Patterns of development in remarried families.* San Francisco: Jossey-Bass.

Pasley, K. (1987). Family boundary ambiguity: Perceptions of adult stepfamily members. In K. Pasley &

M. Ihinger-Tallman (Eds.), *Remarriage and stepparenting: Current research and theory.* New York: Guilford Press.

Pasley, K., Rhoden, L., Visher, E. B., & Visher, J. S. (1996). *Stepfamilies in therapy: Insights from adult stepfamily members.* Manuscript submitted for publication.

Sager, C. J., Brown, H. S., Crohn, H., Engel, T., Rodstein, E., & Walker, L. (1983). *Treating the remarried family.* New York: Brunner/Mazel.

Stern, P. A. (1978). Stepfather families: Integration around child discipline. *Issues in Mental Health Nursing,* 1(2), 50–56.

Visher, E. B. (1994). Lessons from remarriage families. *American Journal of Family Therapy,* 22(4), 327–336.

Visher, E. B., & Visher, J. S. (1979). *Stepfamilies: A guide to working with stepparents and stepchildren.* New York: Brunner/Mazel. (This book is also available in paperback with the title: *Stepfamilies: Myths and realities.* Secaucus, NJ: Carol Publishing Co.)

Visher, E. B., & Visher J. S. (1988). *Old loyalties, new ties: Therapeutic strategies with stepfamilies.* New York: Brunner/Mazel.

Visher, J. S., & Visher, E. B. (1989). Parenting coalitions after remarriage: Dynamics and therapeutic guidelines. *Family Relations,* 38, 65–70.

Visher, J. S., & Visher, E. B. (1990). Dynamics of successful stepfamilies. *Journal of Divorce and Remarriage,* 14, 3–12.

Wallerstein, J. S., & Kelly, J. B. (1980). *Surviving the break up: How children and parents cope with divorce.* New York: Basic Books.

Weston, M. J. (1993, October 29). Presentation to Stepfamily Association Professional Symposium, Lincoln, NE.

White, L. K., & Booth, A. (1985). The quality and stability of remarriages: The role of stepchildren. *American Sociological Review,* 50, 689–698.

Whitehead, B. D. (1993, April). Dan Quayle was right. *Atlantic Monthly,* 27(4), 47–84.

INDEX